Army Regulation 40–657
NAVSUP 4355.4H
MCO P10110.31H

I0415919

Medical Services

Veterinary/Medical Food Safety, Quality Assurance, and Laboratory Service

Departments of the Army,
Navy,
and Marine Corps
Washington, DC
21 January 2005

UNCLASSIFIED

SUMMARY of CHANGE

AR 40–657/NAVSUP 4355.4H/MCO P10110.31H
Veterinary/Medical Food Safety, Quality Assurance, and Laboratory Service

This revision dated 21 January 2005--

o Adds "Worldwide" to the title of the Directory of Sanitarily Approved Food Establishments for Armed Forces Procurement (para 1-4).

o Removes the exemption of foreign establishments previously listed in U.S. Department of Agriculture publication, "Foreign Plants Certified to Export Meat and Poultry to the United States" (para 1-6b).

o Eliminates Table 2-2, Summary of Directory Listing Requirements.

o Creates a provision for establishments to submit a certificate of conformance for an established quality control program, which may be evaluated for reduction in the sanitation audit frequency (para 2-6).

o Revises frequency of sanitation audits to allow for flexibility based on sanitary history of the establishment and the nature of the foods produced or handled. Minimum frequencies are also set for specific food items (para 2-6c(2)).

o Changes the classes of inspection from 9 specific classes to 3 broad categories (para 3-1).

o Adds inspection requirements for the Prime Vendor Program (chapter 3).

o Adds the requirement for an installation support plan (paras 3-3 and 3-4).

o Creates a provision for issue of a Certificate of Serviceability in certain circumstances whereby subsistence is unfit for its original or intended use but still wholesome (para 3-4d(4)).

o Revises previously published functions and responsibilities of the Laboratory Service (para 4-2).

o Creates a new laboratory sampling program that incorporates sampling of food items at both origin and destination (para 5-4).

o Converts MEDCOM Form 404-R (Certificate of Unfitness) to DA Form 7538 (Subsistence Serviceability Certificate), and MEDCOM Form 676-R (Request for Veterinary Laboratory Testing and Food Sample Record) to DA Form 7539.

**Departments of the Army,
Navy,
and Marine Corps
Washington, DC
21 January 2005**

***Army Regulation 40–657
*NAVSUP 4355.4H
*MCO P10110.31H**

Effective 21 February 2005

Medical Services

Veterinary/Medical Food Safety, Quality Assurance, and Laboratory Service

By Order of the Secretaries of the Army and Navy:

PETER J. SCHOOMAKER
General, United States Army
Chief of Staff

Official:

SANDRA R. RILEY
Administrative Assistant to the
Secretary of the Army

D. H. STONE
Rear Admiral, SC, USN
Commander
Naval Supply Systems Command

RICHARD L. KELLY
Deputy Commandant, USMC
Installations and Logistics

History. This publication is a major revision.

Summary. This regulation lists responsibilities for food inspection, gives instructions on the audits of food establishments, explains the policy on sanitary approval requirements, defines the various types of food inspections, defines food recall policies, and directs the laboratory sampling program.

Applicability. This regulation applies to the Active Army and Reserve components of the Army, Navy, Air Force, and Marine Corps. This regulation applies to inspections and audits made at the request of the U.S. Coast Guard under the Interservice Support Agreement. It also applies to the Army National Guard (ARNG). Specific instructions regarding Air Force food inspection procedures contained in AFI 48–116 will be followed for food inspections conducted on Air Force installations. The same food safety/quality assurance standards apply during deployments as in garrison.

Proponent and exception authority. The proponent and exception authority to this regulation is the Office of the Surgeon General, HQDA. The proponent has the authority to approve exceptions or waivers to this regulation that are consistent with controlling law and regulations. The proponent may delegate this approval

authority, in writing, to a division chief with the proponent agency or its direct reporting unit or field operating agency, in the grade of colonel or the civilian equivalent Army Activities may request a waiver to this regulation by providing justification that includes a full analysis of the expected benefit and must include formal review by the activity's senior legal officer. All waiver requests will be endorsed by the commander or senior leader of the requesting activity and forwarded through their higher headquarters to the policy proponent. Refer to AR 25–30 for specific guidance.

Army management control process. This regulation contains management control provisions and identifies key management controls that must be evaluated by Army organizations where applicable. Evaluation of these key management controls by other DOD components is strongly encouraged. If other DOD components elect not to evaluate key management controls identified in this regulation, then evaluation of management controls must be accomplished in accordance with DOD Instruction 5010.38, Management Control (MC) Program.

Supplementation. Supplementation of this regulation and establishment of command and local forms are prohibited without prior approval from HQDA

(DODVSA/OTSG), 5109 Leesburg Pike, Falls Church, VA 22041–3258 (For Army users only.)

Suggested improvements. Users are invited to send comments and suggested improvements on DA Form 2028 (Recommended Changes to Publications and Blank Forms) or related form directly to DODVSA/OTSG, 5109 Leesburg Pike, Falls Church, VA 22041–3258.

Distribution.
Army: This publication is available in electronic media only and is intended for medical activities only at command levels B, C,D, and E for the Active Army and D and E for the Army National Guard (ARNG) and the U.S. Army Reserve (USAR).

Navy: Electronic only via Naval Supply Systems Command directives Web site (Naval Logistics Library) at http://www.nll.navsup navy mil. Order from: Navy Inventory Control Point, COG "I" Material, 700 Robbins Avenue, Philadelphia, PA, 19111–5098.

Copy to: A2A (Department of the Navy Staff Offices (Chief of Information; Judge Advocate General only); A3 (Chief of Naval Operations N84B (Morgantown, WV only); FF1 (6 copies); FHI; FH3; FH5; FH15; FH16; FH26; FKM8; FKM9; FKM13 (Code 790); FKM14 (5

---

*This regulation supersedes AR 40–657/NAVSUPINST 4355.4F/MCO P10110.31G, 6 November 1997, and AR 40–70/NAVSUPINST 4355.6A/MCO 1 0110. 44A, 1 February 1995.

UNCLASSIFIED

copies) FKM 17 FKM 30 (10 copies) 96349–1500 (25 copies).
FT1; FT30 (Attn: Director, MS Schools
(Code 3350)(75 copies) FT 39 (Code
7300 (25 copies); FT51; FT55 (10 copies).

Officer in Charge, Navy Food Management Team, Mayport Naval Station, Box
280021 Mayport FL 32228–0002 (15
copies).

Officer in Charge, Navy Food Management Team, Norfolk Naval Supply Center,
1955 Morris St., Norfolk, VA
23511–3497 (25 copies).

Officer in Charge, Navy Food Manage-
ment Team, Pearl Harbor Naval Supply
Center, Box 300, Bldg. 482, Pearl Harbor,
HI 96860–5300 (25 copies).

Officer in Charge, Navy Food Management Team, San Diego Naval Supply
Center, San Diego, CA 92136–5206 (25
copies).

Navy Food Management Team, Pearl
Harbor, Yokosuka Detachment, U. S. Na-
val Supply Depot, Attn: Code 105–FM,
FISC PSC 473, Box 11, FPO AP

Navy Food Management Team, Norfolk,
New London, Groton Detachment, Naval
Submarine Base, New London Supply
Dept., Box 500, Groton CT 06349–5000
(25 copies).

Navy Food Management Team, San
Diego, FISC Puget Sound 467 W Street,
Naval Supply Center Bremerton WA
98314–5100 (25 copies).

NAVSUP (SUP 0821 (15 copies); 09A;
OOB, 0311, 91; X(61) Miscellaneous activities requiring NAVSUP directives)
(less FT55).

Marine Corps MARCORPS CODES;
10250372), 10800066), 2020004,
2020006, 2020007 (2), 2193009,
2193011, 2193018, 3700002 (2), 4065001
(2), 4090004, 41060064125020,
41250254 1300004 1300034 159001,
4225003, 5308003 (3), 5790010, 6025002
(3), 66000016600003 6901001,
69010026902004696700 7000105,
7000144722501472300017230002
(6), 7230009 (2), 7230020, 7230055 (2),
72561547377007504038504074,
7505008 7592013 (2), 7608001,

76210003762100776210008 645008,
77180007719003772900 737001,
77370027768143778601277 97005,
7801042, 7801043, 8512002.

Headquarters, U.S. Marine Corps, 2 Navy
Annex, Code (LFS-4), Room 1126, Washington, DC 20380 (3 copies)

East Coast Food Management Team,
MCCSSS Marine Corps Base, Box 20041,
Camp Lejeune, NC 28542–0041 (10 cop-
ies).

West Coast Food Management Team,
PSC Box 555228 Marine Corps Base
Camp Pendelton CA 92055–50 (100
copies).

Western Pacific Food Management Team,
Unit 35005, Marine Corps Base, Camp
Butler, JA 96373–5002 (10 copies).

Contents (Listed by paragraph and page number)

Chapter 1
Introduction, *page 1*
Purpose • 1–1, *page 1*
References • 1–2, *page 1*
Explanation of abbreviations and terms • 1–3, *page 1*
Responsibilities • 1–4, *page 1*
Coordination of food procurement inspection activities by veterinary personnel • 1–5, *page 3*
Shipment of food into overseas MACOMs • 1–6, *page 3*
Inspection guidance • 1–7, *page 3*
Imminent health hazard • 1–8, *page 3*

Chapter 2
Sanitation Audits of Commercial Food Establishments, *page 4*
Sanitation auditing personnel • 2–1, *page 4*
Sanitation standards • 2–2, *page 4*
Sanitation approval procedures • 2–3, *page 4*
Sanitation approval requirements for procurement • 2–4, *page 5*
Initial sanitation audits • 2–5, *page 6*
Routine sanitation audits • 2–6, *page 7*
Special sanitation audits • 2–7, *page 8*
Plant suspensions • 2–8, *page 9*
Sanitation audits of establishments other than those of prime contractors • 2–9, *page 9*
Notification by MACOM veterinarians • 2–10, *page 9*

Contents—Continued

Maintenance of records • 2–11, *page 9*
Publication of the Worldwide Directory • 2–12, *page 9*
Distribution of the Worldwide Directory • 2–13, *page 10*
Removal of establishments from Worldwide Directory listing • 2–14, *page 10*
Establishments that may not have to be Worldwide Directory-listed • 2–15, *page 11*
Unsanitary conditions in establishments exempt from Worldwide Directory listing • 2–16, *page 12*
Locally approved food establishment lists • 2–17, *page 12*
Sanitation inspections of contractor carriers • 2–18, *page 12*
Pre-award surveys • 2–19, *page 12*

Chapter 3
Veterinary/Medical Food Inspections, *page 13*

Categories of inspection • 3–1, *page 13*
Origin acceptance inspections (category I) • 3–2, *page 13*
Receipt inspections (category II) • 3–3, *page 14*
Surveillance inspections (category III) • 3–4, *page 15*
DOD hazardous food and nonprescription drug recall program • 3–5, *page 17*
Identification of inspected food • 3–6, *page 17*
Sanitation inspections of military facilities • 3–7, *page 17*

Chapter 4
Veterinary Laboratory Service, *page 18*

Official laboratories • 4–1, *page 18*
Laboratory functions • 4–2, *page 18*
Use of installation laboratories • 4–3, *page 18*
Collection and submission of samples • 4–4, *page 19*

Chapter 5
Subsistence Laboratory Analysis Program, *page 19*

Food safety and quality assurance support • 5–1, *page 19*
Establishments subject to this program • 5–2, *page 19*
Food safety and public health requirements • 5–3, *page 19*
Monitoring concept • 5–4, *page 19*
Sampling procedures • 5–5, *page 20*
Actions taken upon notification of nonconforming laboratory results • 5–6, *page 21*
Suspension of a product or establishment • 5–7, *page 22*
Reinstatement procedures for suspended products • 5–8, *page 22*
Food safety and quality parameters and methods • 5–9, *page 23*
Categories of products • 5–10, *page 23*

Appendixes

A. References, *page 24*

B. Army Veterinary Service Geographic Areas of Responsibility, *page 28*

C. Management Control Evaluation, *page 29*

Table List

Table 2–1: Food class identities, *page 10*
Table B–1: U.S. Army Veterinary Service Geographic Areas of Responsibility, *page 28*

Glossary

Chapter 1
Introduction

1–1. Purpose
This regulation—

a. Defines the food safety and quality assurance mission of the U.S. Army Veterinary Service.

(1) The U.S. Army Veterinary Service will be used to meet the requirements of individual Services and departments.

(2) The U.S. Army Veterinary Service will support the U.S. Navy and U.S. Marine Corps. Qualified Navy and Marine Corps medical department personnel or Air Force public Health personnel may be used to perform these functions if Army veterinary personnel are not available.

b. Prescribes the general policies and procedures to follow in the inspection of food and food establishments used to supply all military forces. Included are interservice and intragovernmental support agreements that will be reached when such agreements are in the best interest of the Services or military forces.

c. Sets forth the procedures for inspection of—

(1) Food procured by local or other procurement activities with appropriated or nonappropriated funds (NAFs).

(2) Food and food establishments in the case of a civilian contractor operating on an installation when foods are not purchased with appropriated funds or NAFs.

(3) Military and civilian food establishments.

d. Defines the responsibilities and functions of the veterinary laboratory service relative to the—

(1) Testing of subsistence, water, and dietary supplements.

(2) Laboratory diagnosis of communicable and zoonotic diseases and conditions of military interest.

1–2. References
Required and related publications and referenced and prescribed forms are listed in appendix A.

1–3. Explanation of abbreviations and terms
Abbreviations and special terms used in this regulation are explained in the glossary.

1–4. Responsibilities

a. The Surgeon General (TSG), Department of the Army (DA). The Surgeon General, will—

(1) Develop uniform, efficient procedures, consistent with other federal agencies, for inspection of all food procured for use by the Armed Forces.

(2) Ensure that veterinary personnel use established procedures to determine if foods are wholesome, food establishments are sanitarily approved, and quality assurance is provided.

(3) Assign veterinary personnel for food inspection support in response to requests from commanders and procurement requirements.

(4) Coordinate responsibilities cited in paragraphs (1), (2), and (3) above with TSGs, Departments of the Navy (DN) and the Air Force (AF), or designated representatives.

(5) Establish the "Worldwide Directory of Sanitarily Approved Food Establishments for Armed Forces Procurement" (short title: "Worldwide Directory").

(6) Resolve interservice coordination problems that cannot be settled at the command level.

(7) Review interservice correspondence on policy and major administrative actions.

(8) Develop uniform efficient procedures for the veterinary laboratory service.

(9) Provide worldwide geographic areas of responsibility for each element of the Army Veterinary Service (app B).

(10) Establish and maintain a Food Risk Evaluation Committee (FREC), which will provide expert guidance to TSG on matters relating to the safety of foods and develop valid, scientific recommendations on the status of food items with respect to the requirement to originate from an approved source.

(11) Establish and maintain a Food and Water Safety Committee (FWSC), which will provide expert guidance to TSG on matters relating to the inspection, testing, and safety of food and water products worldwide.

b. Designated MACOM veterinarians.

(1) *The Commander, U.S. Army Veterinary Command (CDR, VETCOM).* The CDR, VETCOM will—

(a) Supervise the inspection of food establishments by veterinary personnel within the VETCOM area of responsibility (AOR)(table B–1).

(b) Coordinate inspections with other commands and Services through their medical department personnel.

(c) Publish the Worldwide Directory for use in all areas. The Commander, VETCOM is responsible for consolidating the Worldwide Directory. Content and format of the Worldwide Directory are explained in paragraphs 2–12b and c.

(d) Ensure consolidation of annexes to the Worldwide Directory for designated OCONUS regions in the VETCOM area of responsibility. Designated annexes will be at the discretion of the VETCOM Commander and will include information as required in the Worldwide Directory.

(e) Provide administrative, logistical, and budgetary support to the Director, U.S. Army Veterinary Command Food Analysis and Diagnostic Laboratory.

(2) *Overseas Major Army Command (MACOM) veterinarians outside of the United States Army Veterinary Command's (VETCOM) area of responsibility (AOR) (table B–1*   ). These individuals will—

(a) Administer food inspection activities within their AOR through regulations, directives, inter-service agreements, and technical letters.

(b) Publish an approved source annex for food establishments within the command for use in outside continental United States (OCONUS) procurement. This information will be expeditiously transmitted to VETCOM for inclusion in the Worldwide Directory.

(c) Make at least one supervisory visit every 18 to 24 months to locations within their command where veterinary or medical personnel are engaged in food inspection activities. MACOM veterinarians may designate a representative to perform such visits.

(d) Negotiate agreements with staff veterinarians of other commands on areas of food inspection responsibilities.

(e) Inform and coordinate with the combatant command surgeons and preventive medicine (PM) officials on significant veterinary public health issues.

c. Commanders of overseas MACOMs. The commander of each overseas MACOM will—

(1) Coordinate food inspections with other commands and Services through their staff veterinarians.

(2) Supervise food inspections by veterinary personnel within the command through their staff veterinarians.

d. Commandant, U.S. Army Medical Department Center and School (AMEDDC&S). The Commandant, AMEDDC&S, through the Chief, Department of Veterinary Science, will —

(1) Be responsible for the technical training for all U.S. Army veterinary service personnel worldwide in the areas of food safety and quality assurance.

(2) Continuously review, coordinate, and update military sanitary standards and handbooks.

(3) Draft, coordinate, and prepare new military sanitation standards or handbooks for publication as directed by TSG, DA.

e. Director, U.S. Army Veterinary Command Food Analysis and Diagnostic Laboratory. This individual will—

(1) Serve as advisor to the Director, DODVSA, and Commander, VETCOM on all matters pertaining to veterinary laboratory services.

(2) Be responsible for the technical training of all veterinary laboratory officers and key civilian technical personnel at the various VETCOM and major overseas veterinary laboratories.

(3) Conduct training programs for all veterinary personnel who will be engaged in rapid diagnostic testing of subsistence at the unit level.

(4) Be responsible for the standardization of operations and programs of veterinary laboratory services of the various VETCOM and major overseas command veterinary laboratories.

(5) Be responsible for the coordination of food inspection and laboratory programs as they relate to the administration of chapter 5 of this regulation.

(6) Conduct periodic scheduled inspections of each MACOM veterinary laboratory and other authorized laboratories.

(7) Publish technical data letters, standing operating procedures, and laboratory administrative procedures in support of food inspection activities as described in chapters 4 and 5 of this regulation.

(8) Conduct proficiency surveys and use other media as necessary to assure uniformity of veterinary laboratory services.

(9) Maintain a control laboratory for the Armed Forces on all veterinary laboratory matters.

(10) Maintain technical liaison with laboratory experts throughout the world.

(11) Conduct collaborative technical studies among the veterinary laboratories of the Services' medical laboratories as well as other governmental, institutional, and regulatory agency laboratories.

(12) Maintain contractor quality history files in accordance with chapter 5 of this regulation.

f. Veterinary/medical food inspection personnel. These individuals will—

(1) Protect the health of military personnel from foodborne illnesses through food safety inspections.

(2) Conduct inspections and sanitation audits; report data and results according to this regulation.

(3) Coordinate food inspection activities with other veterinary or medical personnel to prevent duplication of effort.

(4) Support procurement agencies through quality assurance and data analysis and provide appropriate recommendations as required to accountable officers.

(5) Coordinate the collection and submission of samples with the appropriate servicing laboratory.

g. Chiefs of major overseas veterinary medical laboratories. These chiefs will—

(1) Provide technical advice to the MACOM veterinarian for the formulation of policies related to the testing phase of the veterinary food inspection service.

(2) Advise the MACOM veterinarian of sanitary defects or epizootics that may be detected through the laboratory examination of materials submitted from the field on a routine basis.

h. Procurement agencies. These will—

(1) Notify MACOM veterinarians through appropriate channels of all contracts awarded for the procurement of food for the Armed Forces and the quality assurance provisions applicable to the contracts.

(2) Provide all proposed changes to food inspection policies and procedures that could—

(a) Have a bearing on health and sanitation.

(b) Require changes in budget or personnel requirements of veterinary or medical personnel.

1–5. Coordination of food procurement inspection activities by veterinary personnel

The responsibility for coordinating food procurement inspection activities includes defining the areas of inspection responsibility for veterinary personnel. The coordination will be accomplished as follows:

a. The CDR, VETCOM, and overseas MACOM veterinarian, outside of VETCOM's AOR, will direct the coordination of origin food inspection activities. The MACOM veterinarians of the commands concerned will determine the areas of responsibility for procurement inspections. An agreement will be reached before changing areas of responsibility. Matters that cannot be resolved between commands will be sent through channels to DOD Veterinary Service Activity (DODVSA), 5109 Leesburg Pike, Falls Church, VA 22041–3258.

b. When possible, coordination of food procurement inspection activities will be decided before annual budgets are prepared. Required inspections will be performed by the least costly means. The command that is to assume responsibility should add any new requirements to its budget.

c. Liaison visits to USA, USN, USAF, or USMC installations by veterinary officers or USAF Public Health officers are encouraged. Veterinary officers will closely coordinate food inspections and listing of food establishments. For coordination purposes, the policy and procedures below apply.

(1) Interservice transmittal of requests for food inspection is encouraged.

(2) Interservice correspondence requesting changes or interpretations of policy as set forth in this regulation will be routed through the appropriate Service listed below.

(a) Army: OTSG, 5109 Leesburg Pike, Falls Church, VA 22041–3258.

(b) Navy: Commanding Officer, Navy Environmental Health Center (Code 38), 2510 Walmer Ave., Norfolk, VA 23513–2617.

(c) Air Force: HQ USAF AFMOA/SGZP, 110 Luke Ave., Room 100, Bolling AFB, Washington, DC 20332–7050.

(d) Marine Corps: Headquarters, United States Marine Corps (Code LFS4), 2 Navy Annex, Washington, DC 20380–1775.

d. Commanders will send requests for food inspection support through command channels to the applicable Service in paragraph c(2) above. The applicable Service will further route the support request to the appropriate location per appendix B. Appendix B identifies the U.S. Army Veterinary Service geographic areas of inspection responsibility.

1–6. Shipment of food into overseas MACOMs

Policy concerning shipment of food into overseas MACOMs is as follows:

a. Veterinary or medical personnel of overseas MACOMs will be informed on import laws and regulations of the countries within their AOR. The Servicing Office of the Staff Judge Advocate will advise the MACOM commanders overseas concerning all laws and regulations to include import laws and regulations.

b. Foreign food establishments may serve as sources of supply only after the MACOM veterinarian determines that local requirements achieve the health and safety standards provided by Federal systems in the United States. Individual plants may be approved, if they meet such standards.

1–7. Inspection guidance

Inspecting personnel will conduct inspections according to this regulation as directed by TSG, DA, and according to guidance in—

a. Part 246, Title 48, Code of Federal Regulations (CFR), requiring the assurance of wholesomeness and quality of food products.

b. Purchase instruments (contracts, blanket purchase agreements, national allowance pricing agreements).

c. Publications such as inspection manuals and instruments of the purchasing agency.

d. Applicable sections of the Federal Acquisition Regulation (FAR) and its supplements.

1–8. Imminent health hazard

a. A product or practice that creates or appears to create an imminent health hazard may be sufficient cause for the immediate suspension of delivery of all involved products until the problem is resolved. Examples include—

(1) A critical establishment sanitary defect, which could likely result in product contamination.

(2) The laboratory-confirmed presence of foodborne pathogens in a product, for which zero tolerance has been established.

(3) A pasteurized product with a positive phosphates reaction.

(4) A pesticide, antibiotic, mycotoxin, or other substance in quantities exceeding authorized limits.

(5) An aseptically processed and packaged milk or milk product that does not meet commercial sterility requirements.

b. The testing laboratory will immediately report laboratory confirmed imminent health hazards to the veterinary unit responsible for sanitation audits of the establishment. That veterinary unit will immediately notify, as appropriate, the contracting officer, prime contractor, subcontractor, and/or regulatory agencies by the most expeditious method. They will also notify the appropriate U.S. state or local health agency with authority over the affected product.

c. Procurement and delivery of that type of product will be suspended. U.S. Government test results indicating nonconformance are cause for rejection of future deliveries of a known nonconforming production lot. However, if a Government contract is involved, the government's response much conform to the terms of the contract.

Chapter 2
Sanitation Audits of Commercial Food Establishments

2–1. Sanitation auditing personnel
Veterinary personnel in the ranks of captain or below, warrant officer, and staff sergeant (SSG) through sergeant major (SGM) must be certified in sanitation audit techniques prior to performing sanitation audits on commercial food establishments. The MACOM veterinarian may require certification of other personnel. The certification process will begin at the AMEDDC&S, will be managed at the Regional Veterinary Command (RVC) or equivalent level, and be implemented to completion at the District Veterinary Command (DVC) or equivalent level. Overseas commanders will determine the level to administer certification. Veterinary personnel will audit the sanitary conditions of food establishments considered for Worldwide Directory listing. When necessary, U.S. Army veterinary and U.S. Air Force public health personnel will also provide sanitation audits for locally approved establishment lists (see para 2–17.). Once certified (as applicable), personnel responsible for audit of food establishments for Worldwide Directory listing are as follows:

a. Veterinary Corps personnel. Veterinary Corps officers (VCO) and warrant officers (WO). Army Veterinary Corps (Doctor of Veterinary Medicine (DVM)/Veterinary Medicine Doctor (VMD)) officers and Veterinary Services Technician (military occupational specialty (MOS) 640A).

b. Army noncommissioned officers (NCOs). NCOs with MOS 91R (Food Inspection Specialist), SSG and above, may perform routine sanitation audits of those food establishments that manipulate/handle packaged foods. Under exceptional circumstances the MACOM veterinarian may authorize these individuals to perform routine sanitation audits on food establishments that process or manipulate/handle unpackaged foods.

c. Veterinary inspection personnel. Veterinary inspection personnel will conduct sanitation audits of commercial ice plants and bottled water plants. When circumstances dictate that water potability certification by the military is necessary, veterinary inspection personnel may draw water samples and submit them to the appropriate Army veterinary laboratory for testing. Results of the tests will be provided to the inspection personnel for use in completing the audit report.

d. Air Force public health personnel. Air Force public health personnel, in accordance with AFI 48–116, will perform inspections/audits of food on Air Force bases. They also will provide inspections/audits for Air Force locally approved establishment lists (see para 2–17).

2–2. Sanitation standards
The documents used for the sanitation audit of food establishments are as follows:

a. The general sanitation requirements for establishments furnishing food to the Armed Forces are found in the latest revision of MIL–STD–3006 and methods for auditing are contained in MIL–HDBK–3006. The sanitation standard listed has appendices with checklists for each commodity. (Each of these checklists may be reproduced locally.) Electronically produced checklists are authorized and encouraged.

b. Additional sanitation documents for establishments furnishing food to the Armed Forces are found in MIL–HDBK 154; USPHS publication 229; Journal of Food Protection Publications 3A and E–3–A; and the United States Public Health Service (USPHS) Publication No. 33: National Shellfish Sanitation Service Publication Program Manual of Operations, Parts I and II.

2–3. Sanitation approval procedures
The MACOM veterinarian, in whose area the food establishment is located, will decide if and when the establishment will be approved for central procurement. Information to review in the determination will include—

a. Reports of sanitation audits.

b. Evaluation of reports in accordance with the applicable Service regulations.

c. Auditor recommendations.

d. Subsequent endorsements by the veterinary commanders of intermediate headquarters recommending approval or disapproval.

2–4. Sanitation approval requirements for procurement

a. Commercial food establishments. All food establishments and distributors are subject to sanitation approval and surveillance as deemed necessary by the CDR, VETCOM; the overseas MACOM veterinarian outside of VETCOM's AOR; or an appropriate Air Force public health authority. Purchasing activities of the Armed Forces will buy foods only from Worldwide Directory listed or locally approved establishments. Suppliers must be sanitarily approved for listing in any directory/local list or be exempt, as defined below, before a contract is awarded or renewed. The only authorized exceptions are—

(1) Establishments referenced in paragraphs 2–15a(2)(a) through (i).

(2) Establishments approved by military entrance processing stations. This exception does not apply to those military entrance processing stations located within the boundaries of a military installation.

(3) On overseas military installations, a dining facility established for the use of local national employees and their guests (German kantines, Italian mensas, and so forth) may be exempt as directed by the responsible local commander. The commander will consult with the supporting medical authority prior to making the decision.

(4) Products of foreign origin purchased in an emergency by the afloat U.S. Navy from unapproved sources. The quantities procured will be strictly limited to the immediate requirements in order to alleviate the emergency. The senior medical department representative will be informed when these purchases are contemplated so that inspection requirements may be established.

b. Off-post caterers and civilian restaurants. These establishments, furnishing meals purchased with appropriated or NAF funds must have sanitary approval to include use of approved sources for food items and ingredients used in meals prepared and served. For one-time occasions, one-time approval is appropriate and Directory or local listing is not necessary. The PM personnel may assist in determining the sanitary status by coordinating with the local health authorities or performing a site visit as appropriate. These or similar off-post establishments should be inspected in accordance with MIL–STD 3006. The Air Force will inspect these facilities in accordance with the Food and Drug Administration (FDA) Food Code. For OCONUS areas, the CDR, VETCOM; overseas MACOM veterinarian outside of VETCOM's AOR; or appropriate Air Force public health authority will develop supplemental guidance for inspectors assessing the risk associated with consuming meals from these facilities.

c. Home delivery service. Commercial food establishments providing home delivery service to individuals residing on a military installation are exempt from sanitation audit and Worldwide Directory or local list requirements of this regulation. Local medical command policy will apply in these instances.

d. Dinner theaters. Directory or local listing of civilian caterers furnishing meals to a NAF-operated dinner theater on a military installation is required.

e. Unit parties. A civilian caterer furnishing meals to a military unit for a unit party or picnic (using NAF morale and welfare funds) must have sanitary approval. For one-time occasions, one-time approval is appropriate and Directory or local listing is not necessary.

f. On-post retail grocery store, restaurant, and fast-food outlets. These or similar on-post establishments are subject to military sanitary inspection and approval. However, Directory or local listing is not required. Inspectors will regard these establishments as similar to military facilities. Retail grocery stores are subject to the same sanitary standards as military commissary stores. The veterinary service will inspect on-post retail grocery stores. Usually, the preventive medicine service is responsible for sanitary evaluation of on-post food service type establishments. Resale grocery items and raw materials for restaurants and/or fast-food outlets must comply with the approved source requirements of this regulation.

g. Mobile canteens and/or snack trucks servicing military installations. These units, when performing under a Government contract, are subject to sanitation audits and Directory or local list requirements as provided in the contract. When the mobile unit operates as an extension of a central food preparation establishment, the base and mobile unit must be audited. Resale food items and raw materials must comply with the approved source requirements of this regulation. The mobile units operating on-post are subject to veterinary and/or preventive medicine service audits. Coordination between veterinary and preventive medicine services is essential to establish responsibility for audits. When operating on-post permissively (without a Government contract), local command policy and requirements for audits and approval will govern. The veterinary service will coordinate with the preventive medicine service to carry out the local command policy. Whether these units are performing under a Government contract or permissively, the local VETCOM should maintain sanitary cognizance.

h. Privately prepared foods. Sanitation audits and Directory or local listing requirements do not apply to food prepared in military quarters or private residences for the following purposes:

(1) In the Air Force, direct sale to individuals requires installation commander's approval and a public health inspection.

(2) Donation to charitable organizations.

(3) Consumption at social gatherings not involving the use of appropriated funds (APFs) or NAFs. Local command policy will apply in these cases.

(4) Military quarters or private residences will not be approved as sources of food for purchase by APF or NAF activities. However, a food processing establishment adjacent or attached to a private residence must be completely separated by a wall or floor for approval as an acceptable source. The food processing establishment must not be an integral part of the residence.

i. Installation events. For air shows, festivals, and similar installation events, veterinary and preventive medicine personnel will retain sanitary oversight but the requirement for the food provided by nonmilitary vendors to come from approved sources may be exempt at the discretion of the installation commander. The installation commander must consult with the supporting medical or veterinary activity prior to determining a course of action. Army publication TB MED 530 contains specific requirements for temporary food service operations at Army installations.

j. Establishments under food safety surveillance. These are establishments that do not require formal sanitation audit approval but are required by the MACOM veterinarian to be listed in the Worldwide Directory in order to serve as a source for Armed Forces procurement.

(1) Food safety surveillance visits (FSSV) will be made to establishments under food safety surveillance on an annual basis (at minimum). More frequent visits will be made at the discretion of the DVC Commander or equivalent level. MIL–HBK 3006 and associated working papers will be utilized to review the establishment. There will be no official scoring, nor pass/fail rating given. Major defects and observations will be annotated and discussed. Food safety concerns or deficiencies will be reported to other relevant inspection agencies (FDA/state/and so forth), as well as through normal command channels.

(2) Listing in the Worldwide Directory will be in a separate category. This area will be designated as Establishments Under Food Safety Surveillance.

(3) Results of visits will be Continued Listing, unless imminent health hazards were noted (process controls, and so forth), at which time temporary suspension status will be invoked. Reports of visits will be distributed in accordance with this regulation.

k. Consumer notification. If a commander exempts a food establishment or facility from the requirements of sanitation approval and the use of approved sources of supply as referenced in paragraph 2–4a(3), he or she will ensure consumer awareness of risk. Consumer awareness programs will include information on potential food safety risks and traveler's food safety advisories (OCONUS) and can be accomplished through various media, such as normal community publications, posting of advisory signs, and newcomer briefings.

2–5. Initial sanitation audits

Initial sanitation audits will be performed according to the guidance given below.

a. Purpose of initial sanitation audits. Initial sanitation audits determine the sanitary status of commercial food establishments for the first time. These audits approve or disapprove the establishments as sources for the Armed Forces. Initial sanitation audits are complete sanitation audits of the facilities, production procedures, and sanitary control systems of the establishment.

b. Requests for initial sanitation audits. Requests for initial sanitation audits will be made as follows:

(1) Suppliers will send their inspection/audit requests directly to the procurement officer of the installation or agency concerned. Written requests for initial sanitation audits from suppliers must be signed by the plant owner or authorized representative. This requirement also applies to requests concerning NAF activities.

(2) The procurement officer will——

(a) Review current approved source documents to determine that the cost associated with the additional listing is in the best financial interest of the government.

(b) Review the request to decide if the firm is otherwise eligible.

(c) Decide if the installation or agency wants to buy the firm's products.

(3) A written request will be prepared and forwarded by the procurement officer to the appropriate activity listed in table B–1. The supplier's request will be attached as an enclosure.

(4) The written request will contain, as a minimum, the following information:

(a) Full name of the establishment, street address (or geographical location), city, state, zip code, and country in which the establishment is located and the mailing address, if different from the location.

(b) Name, title, telephone number, and e-mail address (if available) of the person to be contacted at the supplier's establishment.

(c) Specific products to be furnished (such as breads, rolls, or biscuits), as well as other products being produced.

(d) Establishment number and name of agency if the establishment is currently inspected by the United States Department of Agriculture (USDA), United States Department of Commerce (USDC), or state agency.

(5) Audit requests must be forwarded to the responsible command at least 4 weeks before the results are due. The requests will be processed by the applicable command and sent to the veterinary or medical activity responsible for the audit.

(6) When special circumstances warrant, as determined by the MACOM veterinarian, an initial sanitary audit may be expedited. In such cases, the MACOM veterinarian may act on requests received telephonically from purchasing activities. The followup written request will be processed as described in paragraph (1) through (5) above.

c. Requests for initial re-audit. Requests for initial re-audit will—

(1) Be made in writing and initiated by plant management, within 1 year.

(2) Include a detailed description of the actions taken to correct each deficiency noted during the initial audit.

(3) Be signed by the plant owner or representative.

(4) Be forwarded in accordance with paragraphs 2–5b(1) through (5).

d. Conduct of initial sanitation audits. The guidance used in conducting an initial sanitation audit is as follows:

(1) *Performing the audit.* Initial sanitation audits will be made in the presence of the management (or representative) of the plant. When practical, audits should be coordinated with other inspection agencies (state, county, and city). Production facilities and equipment must be complete and operating at the time of the initial sanitation audit. If appropriate, the audit should begin before or at the end of the day's production so evidence of actual cleanup procedures and efforts can be observed.

(2) *Initial sanitation audit results.* During an exit interview, the auditor making the initial sanitation audit will—

(a) Advise management or its authorized representative of any audit deficiencies found and request corrective action as applicable through a Corrective Action Request (CAR).

(b) Advise management of the normal approval process, based on current MACOM policy, and that final approval authority resides with the MACOM. Ensure management is aware that final approval is not given until acceptable laboratory results are received.

(c) Prepare a written list of deficiencies found during the audit. A copy of this list will be provided to management personnel prior to departure from the plant.

(d) Advise management that the final audit results will be mailed to the company from the MACOM.

(3) *Specific item approval.* Normally, an establishment is approved or disapproved on the basis of all foods produced or supplied with plant equipment and facilities. Even if all of the food items are not found suitable, the establishment may be approved for specific items if the following conditions are met.

(a) The auditing officer finds that processing undesirable items will not affect the approved items.

(b) The processing operations are segregated as if the operations were separate establishments on the same premises.

(4) *Publication results.* The MACOM publishing the approval listing will inform the applicant of the results of the audit (see para 2–10).

e. Initial sanitation audit reports.

(1) Initial sanitation audit reports will contain recommendations for either approval or disapproval. In no case will a "provisional" approval be made. The promise of correcting deficiencies is not grounds for approval. The auditor may withhold recommendations and a final report until the prescribed corrective actions are completed. This action may be taken when time and distance will economically permit the auditor to confirm that corrective actions are completed. A copy of the establishment letterhead or business card will be included with each audit report. A product flow chart including critical control points, when applicable, will be required to be furnished to the auditor. A copy will be submitted as an enclosure to the audit report. In some cases, it may be helpful to include sketches or photographs of specific areas or equipment. Written permission from the management must be obtained before any photographs are taken.

(2) Normally, the audit report will be submitted electronically to the MACOM veterinarian. The audit report will be produced in accordance with MIL–HDBK–3006.

2–6. Routine sanitation audits

Routine sanitation audits will be performed according to the following guidance:

a. Purpose of routine sanitation audits. Routine sanitation audits are made to determine the current sanitary status and overall status of the sanitation program of an establishment listed in the Worldwide Directory. These audits result in the continued approval of the establishment or in notice to its management of the possibility of disapproval if the sanitary deficiencies observed are not corrected in a reasonable amount of time.

b. Directed routine sanitation audits. Routine sanitation audits normally will not be requested, but may be directed by the applicable command if laboratory results indicate a need for increased sanitation cognizance.

c. Conduct of routine sanitation audits. Routine sanitation audits will be performed as follows:

(1) Routine sanitation audits will be complete enough for the auditor to evaluate correctly the current sanitary status and status of the sanitation program of an approved establishment. When the auditor finds serious sanitary deficiencies, he or she will inform the management of the deficiencies. The auditor will, at that time, advise management that the

establishment may be disapproved if the deficiencies are not corrected. Written notice will be given to management as described in paragraph 2–6(e).

(2) Generally, the extent and frequency of audits will depend on the sanitary history of the establishment and the nature of the foods produced or handled. The minimum frequency of routine audits for Worldwide Directory listed establishments will be as follows:

(a) Quarterly: Fresh meat, poultry, seafood, manufactured dairy products, frozen desserts, salad producers, fresh-cut produce, sandwiches, mushrooms, sprouts, and caterers.

(b) Semiannual: Bottled water, ice, and bakeries.

(c) Annual: Shell eggs, seasonal processors during production period, active bidders, commercial warehouses storing Government subsistence, commercial storage/distribution warehouses supplying subsistence for troop feeding (when deemed necessary by the MACOM veterinarian), FSSVs on refrigerated pasteurized juice, and other establishments as required.

(3) All other establishments listed in the Worldwide Directory will be audited on a semi-annual basis.

(4) The minimum frequencies for routine sanitation audits may be reduced by the responsible MACOM veterinarian. The MACOM veterinarian may delegate this authority. This action may be taken when repeated audits show that an establishment is maintaining a highly acceptable sanitary status. An establishment may submit to the MACOM veterinarian, a Certificate of Conformance for an established quality control program that may be evaluated for reduction in the sanitation audit frequency. The frequency of routine audits should increase when audits show that an establishment has relaxed sanitary controls.

(5) The decision to perform unannounced audits will be based upon weaknesses in, or the absence of, a food quality assurance program or improper implementation of current program.

(6) During the exit interview, the auditor will provide management the recommended results of the audit.

d. Exemptions from routine sanitation audits. Plants may be exempted from routine sanitation audits if they require dual listing in the Worldwide Directory and another federal agency inspection directory. The requirement for dual listing includes—

(1) Establishments listed in the USDA publication, "Meat and Poultry Inspection Directory" that produce products not subject to meat and poultry inspection regulations. These products will not bear the mark of a Federal or state inspection. The products are acceptable if they are produced in an area of the plant under sanitary control of a Federal or state inspector and confirmed in writing by the inspector in charge. However, the plants will be dual listed.

(2) International Milk Shippers List (IMSL) plants that produce products not covered by the IMSL product code list (for example, frozen desserts) will be dual listed.

e. Routine sanitation audit report. Routine sanitation audit reports will follow the format and content of MIL–HBK–3006. The auditor will notify an establishment by official memorandum when critical and major deficiencies are observed during a routine audit. This official memorandum will list the deficiencies. A CAR is generated to show corrective actions. The memorandum will also state that a special sanitation audit (determining future approval) will be made after a reasonable length of time. The elapsed time, during which corrections may be made, will—

(1) Be set by the auditor.

(2) Depend on the extent of the deficiencies and the threat to health. As an additional and special reporting requirement, the auditor will report critical deficiencies to the applicable MACOM and procurement agency by telephone, facsimile, or other electronic mail means. (This is an exempt report under AR 335–15, para 5–2b.) Other federal, state, or local health officials will also be notified.

f. Routing of routine audit reports. A copy of the routine audit report will be sent to the MACOM veterinarian.

2–7. Special sanitation audits

Special sanitation audits will be performed according to the guidance below.

a. Purpose of special sanitation audits. Special sanitation audits will be made at an approved plant to decide whether the plant will remain an approved procurement source of subsistence for the Armed Forces. Special sanitation audits are conducted in those food establishments that—

(1) Have a history of marginal compliance with sanitary requirements.

(2) Have had recurring management difficulties.

(3) Have aroused heightened command interests.

(4) Have been determined by veterinary or medical authorities to need auditing.

b. Initiation of special sanitation audits. Special sanitation audits may be initiated—

(1) At the request of the applicable command. The auditor will make a special sanitation audit when it is suspected that food supplied by an establishment is a threat to health.

(2) After a reasonable length of time to correct deficiencies found during a routine sanitation audit.

c. Conduct of special sanitation audits. Special sanitation audits will be focused on the problems found during previous audits that resulted in an unsatisfactory rating. The scope of audit may involve a single process, multiple operations, or the entire facility depending on the nature of the problems identified by previous critical or major deficiencies.

d. Special sanitation audit reports. Special sanitation audit reports will be completed and forwarded to the activity publishing the directory that lists the establishment (see table B–1).

2–8. Plant suspensions

The auditing official will recommend suspension of establishments that have critical deficiencies deemed imminent health hazards. Coordination with the applicable MACOM veterinary headquarters is required.

2–9. Sanitation audits of establishments other than those of prime contractors

Normally, veterinary or medical personnel audit only the establishments that manufacture, process, store, and supply the end food item to be procured. However, there may be a need to audit subcontractors or source plants that supply ingredients or components. The request for a plant audit must come from the subcontractor plant management. The ability to audit subcontractors depends on the terms of the Government's contract with the prime contractor and whether there is a required "flow down" of the audit requirements to the subcontractor.

a. Sanitation audits are required of subcontractors or source plants when—

(1) Ingredients or components are known to have health hazard characteristics.

(2) The prime contractor does not have control procedures needed to detect health hazards normally associated with ingredients or components.

b. Sanitation audits are not required of subcontractors or source plants when—

(1) The end item, ingredient, or component normally does not present a health hazard.

(2) Ingredients or components are under sanitary control of Federal or Federal-state regulatory programs as outlined in paragraphs 2–15a(2)(a) through (i).

2–10. Notification by MACOM veterinarians

The MACOM veterinarian publishing the approval listing will immediately furnish to the management of an establishment a written notice of approval or disapproval after an initial sanitation audit. Concerned procurement agencies and veterinary or medical officers will also be notified. A written notice to procurement agencies and veterinary or medical offices of initial approval of an establishment will state that approval is limited to the products produced after the date of the audit.

2–11. Maintenance of records

The file for each establishment or plant will consist of all sanitation audit reports, official notices, and correspondence on its sanitary status. The veterinary office will maintain a complete file for the establishments audited by the applicable office. The command listing the establishment in its directory will also maintain a complete file.

2–12. Publication of the Worldwide Directory

a. Publication. The Worldwide Directory is consolidated and published by VETCOM. Other MACOMs may continue to maintain a supplement to the Worldwide Directory.

b. Content. The Worldwide Directory will list all food establishments and food distributors, when required, that are approved as sources of supply for the Armed Forces. Brokers and those establishments specifically exempted from the Worldwide Directory listing are described in paragraphs 2–15a(2)(a) through (i).

c. Format. Directories shall adhere to the following general format—

(1) *The name of each establishment.* The names will be listed alphabetically by state or country. Each location audited and approved will be listed separately.

(2) *Product/service provided.* The Worldwide Directory contains a summary of Directory listing requirements by Federal Supply Class (FSC). Products supplied by each establishment will be identified. The FSC (see Table 2–1) of the food may be listed. When an establishment is approved for storage and/or distribution the applicable service provided will be so listed.

(3) *The address of each establishment.* The address will include the exact geographic location (building, number and street, city, state, and ZIP code) of the establishment. A post office box number or other less definitive address is not adequate. If the mailing address differs from the establishment location, the mailing address will be included.

(4) *Inspection responsibility code (IRC) numbers of the veterinary activities conducting audits.* IRCs will be listed for each establishment entry. In addition, a key identifying IRCs by responsible veterinary office will be included as a separate section of the Worldwide Directory.

Table 2-1
Food class identities

FSC: 8905.
Food item: Any combination of meat, poultry, or fish.

FSC: 8910.
Food item: Fresh dairy products. (Fresh dairy products include all items described as mi k products in the Grade A Pasteurized Milk Ordinance, as amended. Cottage cheese, filled and imitation milk products, yogurt mix, and aseptically processed and packaged milk are also included.)

FSC: 8910.
Food item: Frozen desserts. (Frozen desserts include ice cream, mellorine (imitation ice cream), sherbet, ice milk, water ice, ice cream mix, milk shake mix, and other similar frozen desserts, including frozen novelties.)

FSC: 8910.
Food item: Manufactured dairy products. (Manufactured dairy products include cheese, processed cheese, butter, dried mi k, dried skim milk, mi k fat, stabilized sterilized mi k and cream, and sterilized dairy drink. They also include all other dairy foods that are not fresh dairy products or frozen desserts.) (Indicate whether the establishment is approved for cheese prepared from raw milk onl y or for cheese prepared from pasteurized milk.)

FSC: 8910.
Food item: Eggs. FSC: 8915. Food item: Fruits and vegetables.

FSC: 8915.
Food item: Fruits and vegetables.

FSC: 8920.
Food item: Bakery and cereal products.

FSC: 8930.
Food item: Jams, jellies, and preserves.

FSC: 8935.
Food item: Soups and boullions.

FSC: 8940.
Food item: Special dietary foods and food specialty preparations.

FSC: 8945.
Food item: Food oil and fats.

FSC: 8950.
Food item: Condiments and related products

FSC: 8955.
Food item: Cocoa. FSC: 8960. Food item: Beverage, nonalcoholic.

FSC: 8965.
Food item: Beverage, alcoholic.

FSC: 8970.
Food item: Composite food packages.

2-13. Distribution of the Worldwide Directory

The Worldwide Directory will be distributed according to the instructions below.

a. General distribution. The Worldwide Directory can be accessed through the Web. It can be accessed from the VETCOM homepage. (See app A for URL.)

b. Specific distribution. Distribution in hard copy may be made to each military installation having food procurement or sanitation interest, by contacting the U.S. Army Veterinary Command, ATTN: MCVS–FA, 2050 Worth Road, Suite 5, Fort Sam Houston, TX 78234–6005. Telephone: (210)-221–6510.

2-14. Removal of establishments from Worldwide Directory listing

Establishments disapproved for Worldwide Directory listing will be removed from it according to the guidelines below. In all instances, the Directory listing activity publishing that Directory will give written notice, with explanation for removal, to each establishment removed from the Directory listing.

a. Disapproval. When an establishment is disapproved for unsanitary conditions, the command publishing the Worldwide Directory will immediately notify or direct the notification of the concerned procurement agencies and veterinary offices by telephone or e-mail. Telephonic notice will be confirmed in writing. The next daily update to the Worldwide Directory will remove the establishment from Worldwide Directory listing.

b. Inactivity. The commander publishing the Worldwide Directory may, at his or her discretion, remove inactive establishments from the listing. Any establishment that is no longer actively supplying is considered inactive. Based upon local conditions, however, MACOM's should determine their own standards for inactivity. Removal of inactive establishments will not prejudice future Directory listing of these establishments if they are otherwise eligible. Before removing an establishment from the listing, local veterinary personnel will ensure that the establishment is truly inactive as a direct or indirect source. For example, determine if the establishment's products are supplied through a distributor or prime vendor (PV). Establishment officials, sales representatives, and procurement agencies may be consulted prior to removal. The management of an establishment should understand the reason for removal from the Directory listing.

c. Request from vendor. Upon request from the vendor, the establishment will be removed from the Directory listing by the next update.

d. Attainment of eligibility for exemption. When an establishment qualifies as exempt from the Directory listing (paragraphs 2–15a(2)(a) through (i)), it shall be removed by the next update to that Directory.

e. Refusal to allow sanitation audit to be performed or make records available. When a vendor refuses to allow sanitation audit (including official sample collection for laboratory analysis) of his or her establishment or refuses to make sanitation or quality control records available, the establishment may be removed from Worldwide Directory listing. Coordination with responsible contracting agencies must be made at the MACOM veterinarian level to remedy the situation.

2–15. Establishments that may not have to be Worldwide Directory-listed

a. Establishments that may be exempt from Directory listing are of two general types:

(1) Those listed by other Federal agencies and recognized by both the FREC and the MACOM veterinarian as sanitarily approved sources.

(2) Those that produce or handle foods unlikely to present wholesomeness problems. The following food establishments may not have to be listed in the Worldwide Directory:

(a) Establishments listed in the USDA publication, "Hazard Analysis and Critical Control Points (HACCP) Plants Under Federal Inspection." These establishments may serve as sources of food products for those products that bear a Federal or state (if Federal equivalent program) inspection marking. Cold storage warehouses approved by the USDA are not exempt from Directory listing if food owned by the military is stored or handled in the warehouse or establishment. Establishments under state inspection programs certified by the USDA under the Wholesome Poultry Products Act or the Wholesome Meat Act as being "at least equal to" Federal meat or poultry inspection regulations and standards may also serve as sources of meat and meat products or poultry and poultry products. State plants or individual plants are certified separately for meat and poultry. An establishment certified under the Wholesome Meat Act is not authorized to serve as a source of poultry unless also certified under the Wholesome Poultry Product Act, and vice versa. Sources of frozen and dried eggs, poultry, and rabbits (as listed) also are included.

(b) Establishments listed in the USDA publication, "List of Plants Operating Under USDA Poultry and Egg-Grading and Egg Products Inspection Programs." These establishments may serve as sources of shell eggs.

(c) Establishments listed in the "Interstate Milk Shippers (IMS) List" having a pasteurized milk compliance rating of 90 percent or higher and a milk plant compliance rating of 90 or higher, certified by a State milk sanitation officer. This list is published quarterly by the U.S. Food and Drug Administration, 200 C Street, SW, Washington, DC 20204. The establishments listed in the IMS List may serve as sources of—

1. Dairy products indicated by product codes.

2. Flavored drinks and other novelty fluid drinks.

(d) Establishments listed in the USDC Approved List of Fish Establishments and Products. This list is published by the USDC, National Oceanic and Atmospheric Administration, National Marine Fisheries Service, National Seafood Inspection Laboratory. The establishments listed may serve as sources of finned fish products, crabs, and lobsters.

(e) Establishments listed in the Interstate Certified Shellfish Shippers List. This monthly list is published by the U.S. Department of Health and Human Services, Public Health Service, Food and Drug Administration, 200 C Street S.W., Washington, DC, 20204. The establishments may serve as a source of oysters, clams, mussels, and whole or roe-on scallops.

(f) Establishments listed in the "Dairy Plants Surveyed and Approved for USDA Grading Service." This quarterly list is published by the USDA, Agricultural Marketing Service (AMS), Dairy Division, Dairy Grading Section, Washington DC 20250. These establishments may serve as sources of manufactured or processed dairy products by product code. Those establishments denoted with "P" codes (packaging and processing) must be listed in the Directory. When veterinary or medical personnel perform a sanitation audit on a "P" coded establishment providing ungraded products, emphasis will be on determining the source of raw materials being processed and packaged.

(g) Certain foreign establishments whose pre-packed, finished products are imported by distributors or brokers into the United States and sold to Armed Forces procurement agencies for commissary store resale or NAF use do not have to be directory listed. Procurement directly from these sources, without going through U.S. importation, requires that these plants be listed in the Worldwide Directory.

(h) Distributors or warehouses, including cold storage warehouses, storing or handling non-Government-owned perishable or semiperishable food packaged or packed in containers that protect the food from contamination. Overseas MACOMs will list these distributors on their approved lists when it is in the best interest of the Government.

(i) Establishments that only irradiate, with no other food processing on the premises, nongovernment-owned perishable or semiperishable food (re-packaged or packed in containers that protect the food from contamination) are exempt from listing in the Worldwide Directory.

b. The FREC makes recommendations to the director, DODVSA, who acts on behalf of TSG, to exempt from the Worldwide Directory listing specific food products determined to possess little or no potential health hazard. Establishments that produce these products will be exempt from Worldwide Directory listing on an item-by-item basis as determined by the MACOM veterinarian. A summary of Directory listing requirements will be constructed by the MACOM veterinarian for publishing in the Worldwide Directory. For current listings of exempt products, use the Worldwide Directory or particular MACOM listing.

2–16. Unsanitary conditions in establishments exempt from Worldwide Directory listing

a. The exemption of certain categories of food establishments from the Directory listing does not relieve the military services from their basic responsibility to ensure that foods originating from these establishments are wholesome. This is accomplished during the wholesomeness portion of origin, receipt, and surveillance inspections. Commanders will take appropriate action when unsanitary conditions or practices that present a threat to health are brought to their attention.

b. The military services will rely on the listed Federal agency to correct sanitary deficiencies when such establishment is identified in one of their listings (paragraphs 2–15a(2)(a) through (f).). The military services will initiate liaison with that Federal agency at the lowest practical level. If the deficiencies are not corrected by the establishment within a reasonable length of time, the matter will be directed through channels to the applicable military veterinary commander. MACOM veterinarians will inform TSG, DA, of cases in which—

(1) Deficiencies were not corrected at the MACOM level.

(2) Sufficient evidence exists that unsanitary conditions are affecting the wholesomeness of the product.

c. The military services will take action to assure correction of observed or reported sanitary deficiencies in establishments exempted from the Directory listing. These actions may include conducting a special sanitation audit when conditions that present a threat to health are brought to the attention of the applicable commanders. The reasons for sanitation audits may be consumer complaints, requests of contracting officers, adverse condition reports, or other valid reasons. The military services will arrange a liaison with USDA, FDA, or state, county, and municipal officials having an interest in the sanitation of those establishments in which the sanitary status of the establishment prevents production of wholesome products.

2–17. Locally approved food establishment lists

a. Commanders of installations may authorize publication of locally approved food establishment lists. Establishments appearing on local lists will serve as sources only for the installation responsible for their sanitary approval. When an establishment supplies more than one military installation, it will be listed in a Directory and not on a local list. However, an abstract of Directory-listed establishments near an installation may be compiled for use by local procurement personnel along with locally approved lists. Personnel authorized to audit for local lists are the same as those listed in paragraphs 2–1a through 2–1d. The sanitary standards for establishments appearing in a local list will be the same as those in the Directory.

b. Army National Guard state surgeons or their representatives (for example, installation medical officers, veterinarians, preventive medicine officers, and so forth) may allow the establishment of a statewide local list for use by National Guard units only. The sanitary standards for establishments appearing in a local list will be the same as those in the Directory.

2–18. Sanitation inspections of contractor carriers

The sanitary surveillance of vehicles used to transport food is a continuing practice. Normally, surveillance is done when a contractor is actually furnishing or transporting supplies to or from a military installation or storage point. The establishment is responsible for the sanitary control of commercial vehicles used for deliveries to military agencies. Recommendations on the sanitation of vehicles or carriers transporting Government-owned food will be sent to the appropriate contracting agency.

2–19. Pre-award surveys

Pre-award surveys will be conducted according to the guidance given below.

a. Purpose of surveys. Pre-award surveys are made to evaluate a contractor's ability to meet the terms of a proposed contract.

b. Request for surveys. Requests for veterinary or medical personnel to take part in pre-award surveys of food establishments will be prepared and sent by the appointed survey monitor to the appropriate MACOM veterinarian listed in table B–1.

c. Conduct and reports of pre-award surveys. Pre-award surveys will be conducted in accordance with the provisions of the Federal Acquisition Regulation (FAR), Section 9.106 and its Supplements. Veterinary or medical personnel will take part in surveys as requested by the survey monitor.

Chapter 3
Veterinary/Medical Food Inspections

3–1. Categories of inspection
Inspections performed by veterinary service personnel are grouped into three basic categories:

a. Category I - Origin Acceptance Inspections: Acceptance inspections during antemortem, postmortem, at ration assembly plants, and at other food production plants.

b. Category II - Receipt Inspections: Inspection of appropriated and nonappropriated fund deliveries (Defense Commissary Agency (DeCA); prime vendor; exchange; morale, welfare, and recreation (MWR); operational rations, and so forth).

c. Category III - Surveillance Inspections: Inspections conducted at issue points, prior to delivery, and in-storage inspections of all food commodities for all agencies (DeCA; prime vendor; product compliance evaluation (PCEs); exchange; MWR stocks in storage; ship rider program stocks; operational ration unit basic loads (UBLs), and so forth).

3–2. Origin acceptance inspections (category I)
a. Origin acceptance inspections are made at the facilities of the commercial contractor. Origin acceptance inspection of food—

(1) Will be made by veterinary personnel in the continental United States (CONUS) as part of a cooperative training program between DA and other Federal agencies to maintain personnel inspection skills that will be needed in overseas inspections. (The Office of the Surgeon General (OTSG) must approve those personnel taking part in these training programs.)

(2) Will be made by veterinary personnel in CONUS during mobilization or emergency situations when Federal agencies are unable to provide the inspections.

(3) Will be made by veterinary personnel in CONUS at ration assembly plants (meal, ready-to-eat (MRE); unitized group ration (UGR/UGR–A)).

(4) Will be made by U.S. Army veterinary service personnel in overseas areas under the conditions listed below.

(a) On request when food is locally procured by DA, DAF, or DN installations.

(b) On request of a central procurement agency; for example, Defense Supply Center Philadelphia (DSCP), DA, DN, DAF, or exchange procurement activities.

(c) When the MACOM veterinarian decides that wholesomeness factors can be fully determined only during the processing stage.

b. When product deficiencies present imminent health hazards, the inspector will place the product on medical hold, notify the chain of command, and notify the contracting officer of the inspection results. The inspector will also notify the Federal regulatory agency responsible for the product's safety. If the product is wholesome but product characteristics do not meet all contractual requirements, the inspector will notify the contracting officer or his or her representative and recommend rejection based on inspection results. Contracting officer decisions to accept products not meeting contract requirements will be documented on the inspection report and forwarded to procurement and inspection staffs as required by contracting agencies and/or medical authorities.

c. Types of origin acceptance inspections are as follows:

(1) *Antemortem and postmortem inspections.* Antemortem and postmortem inspections are defined as follows:

(a) Antemortem inspections. Antemortem inspection involves the physical examination of live animals before slaughter to detect disease or noxious conditions that would make them unfit for human consumption. Antemortem inspections are needed because there are diseases and conditions hazardous to human health that are best detected in live animals.

(b) Postmortem inspections. Postmortem inspection involves the examination (and testing when required) of carcasses and viscera of animals immediately after slaughter to determine if they are free of diseases or conditions that would make them unfit for human consumption.

(c) Antemortem/postmortem inspection policies. Antemortem and postmortem inspections will be conducted as follows:

1. Domestic animals (including pen raised game (deer, and so forth) and game birds (quail, and so forth) slaughtered for use by the Armed Forces will have antemortem and postmortem inspections. These inspections will be made by veterinary personnel, other Federal agencies, or acceptable state inspection agencies.

2. Wild game mammals or wild game birds for resale or use in troop messes, clubs, or other military food-serving facilities will have postmortem inspections as specified by the MACOM veterinarian.

3. Animals used for survival training are exempt from category I inspections.

4. Animals slaughtered for consumption by U.S. forces (including survival training) must comply with The Humane Slaughter Act, Public Law 85–765, as amended in 1978 by Public Law 95–445.

5. The commanders of overseas MACOMs will provide veterinary personnel to supervise antemortem and postmortem inspections of all animals or poultry slaughtered for use by the Armed Forces. The inspections performed by foreign countries may be approved and accepted at the discretion of the overseas MACOM commander on the recommendation of the MACOM veterinarian. Before making a recommendation, the MACOM veterinarian will thoroughly review the following: applicable regulations, available enforcement procedures, and the qualifications of the inspection such as experience, training, and independence from establishment.

6. The overseas MACOM veterinarian will provide and enforce sanitary standards for foreign slaughtering establishments, issue directives for reporting diseased or unsound carcasses, ensure that diseased or unsound carcasses are not accepted for military use, and coordinate with host nation regulatory authorities as required.

(2) *In plant inspections (ration assembly, food production, and so forth)* In-plant inspections will consist of examining and testing, as needed, contractor-owned food (components, ingredients, and packaging materials).

(a) In-plant inspections are conducted to prevent acceptance of food that is: unwholesome, unsafe, or adulterated; unfit for its intended purpose; a potential danger to health; or in violation of the requirements of other regulatory agencies.

(b) In-plant inspections also protect the financial interests of the Government and NAF activities by determining whether quality factors comply with procurement contracts. Inspections are performed to ensure that food products and the production process comply with the requirements for sanitation, wholesomeness, and condition as well as quality provisions described in the purchase instrument. (Verification and pre-award inspections are included.)

3–3. Receipt inspections (category II)

a. On delivery at purchase (destination) inspection.

(1) The destination inspection is made when food is delivered to the Armed Forces. Food products are inspected to ensure that they comply with the requirements for approved sources, sanitation, wholesomeness, and condition as well as quality provisions described in the purchase instrument. The destination inspection is the last inspection before ownership of food products is transferred to the Government. A documented support plan will be developed by each veterinary unit to ensure receipt inspections are properly managed. The final recommendation to the receiving officer to accept or reject foods will be based on the destination inspection. The authority to reject food items for unwholesomeness rests with the medical authority.

(2) Any food procured by activities such as embassy clubs located on military reservations must be from approved sources and must be inspected by veterinary or medical personnel.

b. Any receipt except purchase inspection.

(1) Government-owned food will be inspected when received from other Government and DOD agencies. This food will also be inspected when received from facilities of a commercial contractor where the product has already been inspected and accepted by the Government. This inspection includes the vehicles in which supplies are transported. The purposes of this inspection are to—

(a) Detect any damage or deterioration that occurred in transit.

(b) Advise receiving officers regarding the conditions of the food's keeping qualities and warehousing requirements.

(c) Detect faulty handling, transportation, or other correctable deficiencies to prevent similar losses in the future.

(d) Verify origin inspection results on free on board (FOB) origin shipments received directly from vendors.

(e) Detect nonconforming products within the warranty period.

(2) Overseas receipt inspections are a unique type of Government-owned inspection. Supplies that are source loaded/transloaded in CONUS for overseas shipment become Government-owned at the port of embarkation. However, the supplies are not normally inspected by the Government before leaving CONUS. These products must be given receipt inspection for contractual compliance upon arrival overseas. Reports of non-conformances at overseas receipt inspection are crucial to warranty action.

c. Nonanimal origin semiperishable foods. Nonanimal origin semiperishable foods such as sugar, salt, and coffee will not normally be inspected upon receipt at military installations. If special circumstances exist or if the procuring agency has filed a specific inspection request, veterinary personnel will inspect these food items before acceptance. When required, infestable subsistence will be inspected in accordance with the current edition of MIL–STD 904.

d. Prime vendor. Deliveries of subsistence supplied to dining facilities, galleys, and any other food activities under the subsistence prime vendor program are subject to inspection upon receipt, but are not normally inspected until after receipt and subsequent placement in storage areas.

e. Exceptions to receipt inspections. Veterinary personnel will provide the final recommendation for all food received for military use except —

(1) At Navy activities, when veterinary inspection food personnel are not assigned.

(a) When food products are received, the food service officer or a designated assistant, or in their absence, a

qualified and responsible person designated in writing by the commanding officer, will inspect the food items for condition, identity, and quantity in accordance with NAVMED P–5010 and NAVSUP P–486.

(b) When food products are received, the receiving individual will also coordinate with the medical department representative. The medical officer or a representative will inspect all food items received directly from contractors to approve their fitness for human consumption.

(2) At Air Force Installations where Air Force Public Health personnel provide on-base food inspection support for Air Force installations in accordance with AFI 48–116.

f. Reporting procedures. Inspection reports will be completed as follows:

(1) *Product inspection reports and technical reports.* Inspection reports of food products will be made as required by military regulations and MACOM directives.

(2) *Certification of receiving reports.* In many locations, the accountable or receiving officer certifies that required inspections have been completed based on inspection reports or DOD Food Inspection Stamped invoices. The DOD Food Inspection Stamp impression on the invoice signifies the product was inspected and conforms to contractual requirements. (Refer to TB MED 263 for use of DOD Food Inspection Stamps.) Veterinary or medical personnel or receiving activity personnel will not prepare or sign acceptance inspection reports or stamp invoices when—

(a) The foods are unwholesome.

(b) Products do not meet contractual requirements. Coordination with local procurement officials is required to determine specific requirements.

(3) *Reports and certificates relative to nonconforming foods.* All nonconforming food products will be reported in accordance with this regulation and applicable MACOM guidance.

(4) *Reports of rejected foods.* Rejection of foods during any category of inspection for unwholesomeness or suspected violation of Federal or state regulations will be reported to the Government agency with regulatory jurisdiction over the product. Failure to report these types of rejections to the appropriate regulatory authority could result in unwholesome food entering the commercial food market or the DOD food market at some later date. Reports will be made to the regional office of the Government agency nearest the destination locations. Reports of rejected foods will be reported as follows:

(a) Rejection reports for meat, meat products, poultry, and poultry products bearing the USDA inspection legend will be made to the appropriate USDA compliance officer. A listing of current USDA compliance officers may be found under regulatory programs in the USDA Food Inspection Service (FSIS) publication entitled "HACCP Plants Under Federal Inspection."

(b) Other types of rejections will be reported to the FDA. A listing of current regional or district FDA offices may be obtained from any district FDA office or by referring to the "FDA Investigations Operation Manual, 2004" Appendix X, "FDA Field Offices and Resident Posts."

(c) All rejection reports involving unwholesome items will be made by the veterinary officer in charge of the inspection office unless other channels of reporting are directed by the MACOM veterinarian. Unwholesome or potentially dangerous items should be reported expeditiously by telephone and confirmed in writing on DD Form 1232 (Quality Assurance Representative's Correspondence). Rejections for other reasons may be reported by mail using DD Form 1232, unless otherwise directed by the MACOM (for example, electronic reporting). When stating a suspected violation of Federal or State regulations, the report will be marked FOR OFFICIAL USE ONLY and handled as an exempt report under AR 335–15, paragraph 5–2b. This report should be in narrative form and contain at least the following data:

1. Name, grade, telephone number, and organization of the veterinary inspector making the report.

2. Contract number, lot number, nomenclature of product, location of product, manufacturing establishment number (USDA, USDC, or State plant number), and the name of the contractor.

3. Quantity, date, time, place, and cause of the rejection.

4. Any other pertinent information.

3–4. Surveillance inspections (category III)

Surveillance inspections are made to determine if Government-owned foods are wholesome and suitable for further storage, shipment, issue, sale, and consumption. These inspections and reports will be conducted in accordance with provisions of AR 40–656/NAVSUPINST 4355.10/MCO 10110.45, or other directives issued by contracting agencies.

a. Surveillance factors. Factors to be considered in making determinations include, but are not limited to the following:

(1) The evidence of actual or potential deterioration or spoilage due to contamination (naturally occurring or intentional) by microorganisms or their toxins.

(2) An exposure to chemicals, radioactive materials, or other foreign matter.

(3) The suitability of the item for the purpose intended.

(4) Aesthetic considerations.

(5) Rodent and/or insect infestations.

b. Surveillance inspections at installations, storage facilities, ships, and activities. Veterinary personnel will conduct surveillance inspections for all types of Government-owned appropriated and nonappropriated fund foods at DA and DN installations, storage facilities, ships, and activities. (See para 3–3e for DN exception procedure.) A documented support plan will be developed by each veterinary unit to ensure surveillance inspections are properly managed.

c. Wholesale stocks. Veterinary personnel will inspect wholesale stocks of food that are under the logistical control of the Defense Logistics Agency (DLA). Veterinary personnel will inspect prepositioned war reserve stocks. These inspections will be made according to this regulation and the directives of the accountable agency.

d. Types of surveillance inspection.

(1) *Prior to shipment inspection.* These inspections are performed immediately before Government-owned subsistence is shipped from one Government installation or accountable officer to another. The inspection is performed to ensure that the product is suitable for shipment and its intended purpose on arrival. This prevents labor, transportation, and subsistence from being wasted, through the shipment of material that is damaged, or deteriorated, or has no value upon arrival. Damage that occurred during commercial storage is also detected and appraised. The conveyance used to transport the food and the loading operations will also be inspected. Inspection prior to shipment will be made on a timely basis avoiding any delays in the shipping schedules. Requirements for inspection may be based on problems identified on receipt or previous surveillance inspection or upon a request from an accountable officer or representative.

(2) *At issue or sale inspections.* Inspections of Government-owned foods are made at the time of issue to troop dining facilities, other Government dining facilities or messes, and after receipt but before sale of food in commissary stores. The inspection will include inspection of the vehicles in which the supplies are to be shipped. Requirements for inspection may be based on problems identified on receipt or other surveillance inspections or upon a request from an accountable officer or representative. Sufficient samples of a product will be inspected to assure that no contaminated, decomposed, or otherwise unwholesome foods are issued or sold. All damaged, outdated, or otherwise distressed products will be inspected to determine fitness for consumption prior to offering for sale or issue. Representative samples may be taken and submitted to the appropriate laboratory. The results of tests performed on these samples will be used to determine the product's serviceability for intended/future use or for advising accountable officers on future procurement/storage practices.

(3) *In-storage inspections.* In-storage inspections are inspections of Government-owned food held in storage or reserve for any appreciable length of time.

(a) In-storage inspections will—

1. Detect early signs of deteriorating food. Any signs of deteriorating food should be reported to the accountable officer. The accountable officer may then make arrangements to issue or otherwise dispose of such food before additional deterioration occurs.

2. Be performed on all infestable items, to include dry pet foods.

3. Not be performed routinely in CONUS on locally stored resale items for the commissary unless storage conditions are such that these inspections would be in the best interest of the Government. Normal rotation practices and warehousing procedures are usually sufficient to rotate stocks. Problem areas of improper stock rotation should be reported to the responsible property officer during sanitation evaluations.

4. Implement Navy policy and procedures for the proper disposition of foods in conjunction with decommissioning, fleet rehabilitation, overhauls, emergency repairs, returning Combat Logistic Force ships, and temporary or permanent closure of dining facilities (see NAVSUP P–486).

(b) In-storage inspections will be made on Army, Navy (ashore and afloat), Marine Corps, and DLA installations, depots, and activities. Accountable officers will identify and request items to be inspected at any location.

(c) More frequent inspections of stocks are necessary if conditions at the storage location are below standards or if requested by the accountable officer. In-storage inspections will be made of all foods centrally stored by DA, DN, or MC activities. NAF and club system food stocks should be inspected if indicated by local conditions and considered to be in the best interest of the Government or upon request by the accountable officer.

(d) Residual stocks resulting from turn-in of unused food items will be inspected upon request for signs of deterioration and distress.

(4) *Prime vendor product compliance evaluations.* Product compliance evaluations will be performed on products delivered to troop dining facilities, galleys, messes, and temporary storage locations. These are normally performed after the items have been received and stored.

e. Recommendations for disposition. Surveillance inspections are advisory in nature. The findings and recommendations for disposition will be presented to the accountable officer according to the guidelines below.

(1) *Criteria.* Appropriate dispositions will be recommended (in writing) to the accountable officer when either paragraph (a) or (b) below apply—

(a) Food has deteriorated but is usable.

(b) Preventive or corrective action is needed to avoid further deterioration and loss.

(2) *Examples of disposition.* Examples of appropriate disposition include transfer, turn-in, early issue, forced issue (see AR 30–22 or NAVSUP P–486), reworking, further inspection, or laboratory testing.

(3) *Subsistence serviceability certificate.* Veterinary personnel may determine through surveillance inspection that the food is unfit for human consumption or its intended purposes. If so, a subsistence serviceability certificate will be issued. DA Form 7538 (Subsistence Serviceability Certificate) will be utilized, except that Army inspectors at troop issue subsistence activities will use the documentation prescribed by AR 30–22. Air Force activities will document and report nonconforming food inspection results in accordance with AFI 48–116. If specific instructions for defining unfitness are not prescribed, the certificate of unfitness will include one of the following statements:

   (a) The subsistence items listed above are unfit for their original or intended purpose; however, the product is still wholesome and may be retained for alternative use.

   (b) The subsistence items listed above are unfit for human consumption, and create a health or safety hazard within the facility. Disposition by immediate destruction is recommended.

(4) *Certificate of Serviceability.* In certain situations, the condition of food items may not be fit for their original or intended purpose, but is still wholesome and may retain value for an alternative use. A DD Form 1232, memorandum (or electronically generated certificate) may be issued to the food activity stating: "The subsistence items listed are wholesome, but do not meet the requirements associated with their original purpose or intent for use. They possess value for alternative uses."

(5) *Circumstances of loss or condemnation.* In addition to the information in paragraph (3) above, written details of the circumstances surrounding loss or condemnation will be included on the certificate of unfitness. For insect infestation, give pertinent information including the date the product was received, length of time in storage, appearance of the product according to previous surveillance inspection reports, and recommendations at that time. Submit DD Form 1222 (Request for and Results of Tests) to a military entomology laboratory as per MIL–STD 904, and DSCP Manual 4155.6.

(6) *Unfitness procedures.* The accountable property officer should contact the local DRMO to make sure that unfit food is not saleable for some other purpose. For example, unfit food may be sold for animal foods or to manufacturers of soap, candles, and fertilizers. The veterinary officer will ensure that the quantities shown on the certificate of unfitness are the same as the amounts inspected and found unfit.

(7) *Disposal of unfit food.* The Defense Revitalization and Marketing Office (DRMO) will dispose of unfit food based on the guidance in DOD 4160.21–M. If the unfit food creates a public health hazard, the veterinary officer will give technical advice to the DRMO as needed on the denaturing, disposal, and destruction of food that is unfit for human consumption or its intended purpose. Veterinary personnel will not witness or certify the destruction of unfit food.

(8) *Method of destruction.* Normally, the veterinary officer will not recommend the method of destruction of unfit food. However, when the veterinary officer decides that unfit food is a public health hazard and requires disposal, he or she will make separate written recommendations for the method of disposal to the DRMO. The accountable officer will ensure that all unfit food is segregated and marked as unfit until its disposal.

   f. *Reporting of surveillance inspections.*

(1) Surveillance inspections will be reported according to AFI 48–116, AR 40–656/NAVSUPINST 4355.10/MCO 10110.45, AR 30–22, MIL–STD 904, DPSCM 4155.43, and directives issued by the accountable agency (such as DN, DLA, DSCP, DeCA, and Exchange Service).

(2) Surveillance inspection will be made according to AFI 48–116 AR 40–656/NAVSUPINST 4355.10/ MCO10110.45, AR 30–22, MIL–STD 904, DPSCM 4155.43, guidelines issued from the MACOM veterinarian and/or directives issued by the accountable agency (that is, DN, DLA, DSCP, DeCA, and Exchange Service).

3–5. DOD hazardous food and nonprescription drug recall program

   a. ALFOODACT inspections will be made according to DLAR 4155.26/AR 40–660/NAVSUPINST 10110.8C/AFR 48–116/MCO 10110.38C.

   b. If a food item is suspected to contain a potentially hazardous condition or during an investigation of a customer complaint, a hazardous condition is discovered, the DSCP Consumer Safety Officer must be notified immediately.

3–6. Identification of inspected food

Veterinary or medical personnel will identify inspected food with DOD procurement and surveillance inspection medical service stamps, when required. These inspection stamps will be applied to food items in accordance with TB MED 263, AFI 48–116, or as directed by the procurement/accountable agency.

3–7. Sanitation inspections of military facilities

   a. Sanitation inspections will be made on all military facilities storing or displaying subsistence. This includes commissaries, PX/BX Marts, NEX Marts, exchange facilities, cook/chill facilities, and MWR activities. In DeCA facilities (except on Air Force bases), all processing and food preparation areas will be inspected by Army veterinary personnel.

   b. Frequencies of inspections will be determined by MACOM directives.

   c. The FDA Food Code will be used for all commissary and exchange service facility inspections. MIL–STD–3006, appendix A, will be used for Government warehouse (troop issue subsistence activity, child development center, and so forth) sanitation inspections.

Chapter 4
Veterinary Laboratory Service

4–1. Official laboratories
Official laboratories furnishing laboratory services for food are as follows:

a. The VETCOM Food Analysis and Diagnostic Laboratory, Fort Sam Houston, TX, 78234.

b. The Veterinary Laboratory-Europe, CMR 403, Landstuhl, Germany, APO AE 09180.

c. USPHS laboratories and those state, county, city, and municipal laboratories approved by the USPHS for the wholesomeness testing of fresh dairy products. Approved laboratories are listed in the current edition of the FDA's IMS List.

d. Other laboratories as individually authorized by TSG, DA, according to the provisions of paragraph 4–3.

e. The Navy Environmental and Preventive Medicine units listed below (limited food laboratory support).

(1) Navy Environmental and Preventive Medicine Unit No. 2, Norfolk, VA 23511–6288, Commercial: (804) 444–7671, DSN: 564–7671.

(2) Navy Environmental and Preventive Medicine Unit No. 5, Naval Station, Box 143, San Diego, CA 92136–5143, Commercial: (619) 696–6130, DSN: 958–6130.

(3) Navy Environmental and Preventive Medicine Unit No. 6, Box 112, Pearl Harbor, HI 96960–5040, Commercial: (808) 471–9505, DSN: 430–0111, ext 9505.

(4) U.S. Navy Environmental and Preventive Medicine Unit No. 7, Naples, Italy, Mailing address: Box 41, FPO New York 09521–4200, DSN: 625–1110, ext 4499.

4–2. Laboratory functions
Veterinary laboratory services of the VETCOM and major overseas medical laboratories include the following functions:

a. Conduct microbiological, chemical, toxicological, and radiological analysis of subsistence, nonprescription drugs, water, dietary supplements, and cosmetics to assist submitting inspectors to determine their—

(1) Fitness for consumption, issue, or resale.

(2) Conformance with contractual requirements, within the scope of the laboratory certification and capabilities.

b. Conduct technical inspections of overseas contractor's in-plant laboratories within establishments supplying products for the Armed Forces, at the discretion of the MACOM veterinarian.

c. Training military and civilian personnel in veterinary laboratory procedures.

d. Maintain liaison with various laboratories to obtain and disseminate technical information on veterinary problems peculiar to the area. This includes commercial, Federal, state, city, county, educational institutions, or laboratories of foreign or host countries. Technical data obtained is for information purposes only.

e. Perform analysis of subsistence for contract compliance. When conducting these tests the veterinary laboratory must use only those procedures designated in contractual documents. The methods of analysis obtained from other sources that are determined superior to those designated in contractual documents will be submitted to the VETCOM Food Analysis and Diagnostic Laboratory for review and recommendation.

4–3. Use of installation laboratories
a. Authorization. Laboratory facilities located at U.S. military installations or elsewhere may be used for the testing of fresh dairy foods or other substances when authorized by the CDR, VETCOM, or MACOM surgeon. These authorized laboratories may be used for the quality and sanitary control of fresh dairy food delivered to installations, which will be based on the recommendations of the officers performing surveys prescribed by paragraph 1–4f. The scope of the authorizations will be stated. For example, state whether the testing is unofficial testing for all requirements instead of what is to be performed in official laboratories.

b. Supervision. For purposes of making these tests, authorized installation laboratories will be under the technical supervision of the director of the veterinary laboratory service of the applicable official laboratory. This supervision will consist of, but not be limited to, the following:

(1) An annual technical inspection of each laboratory by the laboratory officer or his or her representative from the official control laboratory.

(2) Proficiency surveys.

(3) Training of personnel.

(4) Exception to this supervision occurs when the laboratory is approved by another recognized quality assurance (QA) system that meets the specific approval of the director, VETCOM lab.

4–4. Collection and submission of samples

a. U.S. Army veterinary personnel will collect and submit samples and specimens according to the instructions contained in the VETCOM Food Analysis and Diagnostic Laboratory Sample Submission Guide.

(1) Samples of fresh dairy foods may be sent to those laboratories authorized in paragraphs 4–1 and 4–3 to perform such analyses.

(2) Samples will be collected and submitted as frequently as necessary to assure that proper laboratory support and control agrees with the mission of the Army veterinary service. Samples will be tested unless—

(a) Requests for unusual analysis, determination, or the testing of excessive numbers of samples are made. Requests may be denied by the receiving laboratory after consulting with the MACOM veterinarian.

(b) The investigation reveals that requests are impractical or nonessential. The director of the official laboratory, at his or her discretion, may apply reduced frequency testing schedules for the samples submitted or delete requests in their entirety after consultation with the MACOM veterinarian. When the above actions are taken, the director of the receiving laboratory will notify the submitting installation.

(c) The samples cannot be tested due to a lack of equipment or other technical reasons. The receiving laboratory may forward or direct referral of those samples to a laboratory that is capable of performing the required testing.

b. The laboratory request form is DA Form 7539 (Request for Veterinary Laboratory Testing, and Food Sample Record) and/or DD Form 1222 .

Chapter 5
Subsistence Laboratory Analysis Program

5–1. Food safety and quality assurance support

This chapter outlines sampling procedures and techniques in support of the Food Safety and Quality Assurance (QA) programs. These procedures form an integral part of the overall mission of protecting military personnel and DOD beneficiary populations from foodborne illness. This chapter prescribes the methods and procedures used to determine compliance with laboratory requirements, and describes the concept and design for a laboratory sampling program targeted at potentially hazardous foods (PHFs). The program allows for testing of those PHFs inspected in accordance with other U.S. Federal or state agency programs. Laboratory testing includes pathogenic and nonpathogenic bacteria, as well as other wholesomeness and quality parameters. A list of products requiring sampling during sanitation audits and their corresponding microbiological criteria is contained in the Worldwide Directory.

5–2. Establishments subject to this program

The provisions of this regulation and this chapter are applicable to commercial and Government food establishments providing subsistence to the Armed Forces; DeCA; MWR; Air Force services; Military Exchange service operated facilities; and dining facilities receiving PV items. Contracts with commercial establishments should contain provisions reflecting these requirements. Selection of samples from retail/user level facilities located on U.S. Air Force installations depends upon the management of that facility. Facilities operated on U.S. Air Force installations that are solely subject to sanitation and public health policies of U.S. Air Force Public Health may be included in this program. Coordination between the district/detachment level veterinary commander and the appropriate public health officer on the U.S. Air Force installation is required. Army veterinary/medical food inspection personnel will be utilized whenever practical to perform this mission.

5–3. Food safety and public health requirements

a. Establishments listed in the Worldwide Directory are required contractually to test for specific pathogens in those PHFs identified by TSG to be of significant public health concern. This end-item testing will be performed by an independent laboratory at the establishment's expense.

b. For each PHF identified by TSG as a significant public health concern, subsistence contracting agencies shall include wholesomeness requirements, to include their applicable limits, in each contract. These requirements will not be a substitute for, nor waiver to, formal sanitation audits that may be otherwise required.

5–4. Monitoring concept

a. This is a three-part program, consisting of the following sampling methods.

(1) *Sanitation audit sampling.* Sampling of food items at their place of manufacture (origin) as part of the sanitation audit program. This includes selecting samples during initial and special sanitation audits, and if directed by the MACOM veterinarian, during performance of directed routine audits. Establishments failing to attain acceptable sanitation compliance will not have samples submitted for analysis. Samples may be selected during normal routine

audits if valid public health concerns indicate a need to do so. Examples of such concerns include but are not limited to the following:

(a) Nonconforming lab results are noted in the establishment's records without identification of the cause or without acceptable resolution of the cause.

(b) Nonconforming lab results showing trends that indicate an establishment's system and processes are out of control.

(c) Other evidence or signs noted during the sanitation audit that indicate the potential for contaminated final product. The auditor's unit commander and the MACOM veterinary laboratory will be notified when such sampling occurs. Justification for sampling will be listed on the audit report.

(2) *Other origin sampling.* Origin sampling of food items and products may be necessary at times other than in conjunction with a sanitation audit. The MACOM veterinarian will determine when such circumstances exist and will coordinate the sampling plan and procedures with procurement agencies and the MACOM veterinary laboratory.

(3) *Destination monitoring sampling.*

(a) Destination sampling of food items. As part of an overall product monitoring program and to monitor their safety and quality, products are sampled from Government establishments or facilities under the direction of the Director of the MACOM Veterinary Laboratory. Establishments or facilities where sampling will occur include-

1. Commissary operations/departments.
2. Military exchange activities.
3. MWR activities.
4. Prime vendor/troop feeding facilities.

Food products originating from establishments under direct in-plant inspection by U.S. Federal authorities (FDA, USDA, USDC, or U.S. Federally recognized state authorities) will be sampled and tested based upon customer complaints or other valid public health reasons. Destination sampling will also include items produced by, or destined to, other Government appropriated and nonappropriated fund food procurement and retail agencies (DeCA, Army and Air Force Exchange Services (AAFES), Navy Exchange(NEX), PV, Air Force Services, and MWR activities). To preclude supply failure, food items destined for dining halls under the prime vendor program may be sampled after prior coordination/agreement between the particular dining facility and the local veterinary unit. Food items that are prepared by dining facilities (salads, meals, and so forth) are not included as part of the monitoring program, but may be sampled if requested by the food service authority.

(b) Responsibilities. The accountable officer or designated representative is responsible for—

1. Ensuring the products are made available for sampling.

2. If appropriate, initiating corrective actions when notified by veterinary/medical food inspectors of nonconforming laboratory test results. When applicable, notify the next higher organizational level (for example, DeCA regional office, AAFES, DSCP, or Army Center of Excellence Subsistence (ACES)) when analyses reveal situations affecting food distribution, storage, or public health.

b. The Army Veterinary Service reserves the right to sample any food item in connection with suspected foodborne disease outbreak investigations, or for other valid public health related problems or concerns. When specific quality requirements are prescribed in the purchase instrument, samples may be submitted for analysis as required. In general, aerobic plate counts (APC) or standard plate counts (SPC) are used as an indication of sanitation and food handling practices within a food production system and may denote an increased probability for pathogenic bacteria. Samples exceeding normal tolerances for non-pathogenic organisms may be used to determine contractor quality history and possibly result in a routine audit being directed by the MACOM veterinarian. Nonconformances of this nature require the DVC/unit commander to coordinate/determine the best course of action within 72 hours of receipt of nonconforming reports. The MACOM approved sources division and MACOM veterinary laboratory will be notified of actions taken.

5–5. Sampling procedures

a. Sampling during the performance of a sanitation audit.

(1) For production lot sizes of 150 or more, 10 samples will be selected. For homogeneous production lots (for example, ice cream, bagged ice) only 5 samples will be selected. For production lots of less than 150, 5 samples will be selected. Homogeneous lots are those that are continuous production of the sample type/style of product and should be sampled during production. There is no requirement to submit final packages of large/bulk pack items (for example, 10 lbs. of bagged ice). Five samples of bagged ice, randomly selected during production and specifically packed in smaller containers may be obtained for the purpose of this regulation.

(2) When selecting samples, products may be grouped, but stratified sampling will be used to ensure a fair representation of all varieties produced. Auditors will consider different production lines, processes, product types and varieties, when stratifying their samples.

(3) To the extent possible, when sampling is performed during a special sanitation audit, it will be limited in scope to the problem area that generated the special audit. If a routine audit is directed by the MACOM veterinarian (directed routine), sampling will be performed on like items that have been identified during the surveillance monitoring

program and have laboratory results that indicated a sanitation problem may exist in the production of that item. If the samples submitted as part of the initial sanitation audit are conforming, no further laboratory testing is required in order to approve the establishment for Directory listing.

    b. Sampling as part of the destination/origin monitoring program.

    (1) Monitoring of PHFs (including ready-to-eat products) is accomplished by selecting samples at destination (for example commissary, shoppette, dining hall, snack bar, and so forth), or origin, as directed by the director, MACOM veterinary laboratory.

    (2) Regardless of source, representative sampling is directed. This means that enough small samples covering the wide range of brands offered are represented. This may require multiple samples to be submitted. Samples will be protected against any significant change that would affect test results during the interval between collection and laboratory analysis. Use aseptic sampling procedures at all times to eliminate any possibility of sample adulteration. Samples should originate from the smallest intact retail containers available, or from aseptically collected non-intact samples. A label from each aseptically sampled product with full item nomenclature including ingredients is required.

    (3) All sampling will be recorded in a vendor performance file and will be maintained at the unit level. Results of laboratory analysis, sample receipts, customer complaints, and corrective action notices will be included in each vendor performance file.

    (4) Contractor quality history records are maintained by the MACOM laboratory utilizing DD Form 2385 (Microbial Quality History Record).

    (5) RVCs/equivalent will manage the program to ensure that sampling is performed in accordance with the direction of the MACOM Laboratory Director.

    (6) Within each DVC/unit samples will be selected from a variety of different bases, installations, and/or retail outlets, in accordance with the direction of the MACOM Laboratory Director.

5–6. Actions taken upon notification of nonconforming laboratory results

    a. Samples containing pathogens or adulterants.

    (1) If pathogens or adulterants, as defined by current federal food safety regulations and standards, are discovered as part of an initial sanitation audit, the establishment is disapproved based upon laboratory results, even if found to be otherwise acceptable.

    (2) If pathogens or adulterants are discovered as part of a special sanitation audit that is otherwise scored satisfactory, or a directed routine sanitation audit, the product will be suspended. If the particular public health problem cannot be isolated to one production method or process independent of other establishment operations, the entire establishment will be suspended. Procedures outlined in paragraph 5–8 will be followed to reinstate the establishment or product.

    (3) If pathogens or adulterants are discovered as part of the origin monitoring program—

    (a) Within 24 hours.

    1. The producing establishment will be notified of lab results by the veterinary unit with sanitation audit responsibility.

    2. The appropriate public health regulatory authority and purchasing agency will be notified by the unit that selected the origin sample. As applicable, the appropriate food safety office (DSCP consumer safety officer, and so forth) will be notified if a recall action is required after the audit.

    3. The responsible veterinary unit commander notifies the MACOM veterinarian.

    (b) Within 48 hours.

    1. If the establishment is listed in the Worldwide Directory, a routine sanitation audit will be scheduled to investigate the source of the problem. The audit is focused on the particular item and its production method.

    2. The results of the audit will determine if a medical hold action will be expanded to other lots and if suspension of deliveries for all lots/items/products will be initiated.

    3. The results of the audit and the recommendation of the auditor will be telephoned to the MACOM veterinarian.

    4. If the producer is under the sanitation cognizance of another Federal agency, that agency must be notified by the unit selecting origin samples.

    5. If products are suspended, three consecutive conforming test results from three different production lots are required to reinstate the product and/or manage the final disposition of medical hold items. All samples must be pulled at origin by the establishment and testing conducted by an accredited commercial laboratory at the establishment's expense. The MACOM laboratory will verify and validate all laboratory results.

    (4) If pathogens or adulterants are discovered as part of the Destination Monitoring Program (vendor produced and delivered items)—

    (a) Within 24 hours.

    1. Products found to contain pathogenic microorganisms or adulterants will immediately be placed on medical hold.

    2. The destination unit finding the problem will notify the veterinary unit responsible for sanitation audits of the establishment.

3. The producing establishment will be notified of lab results by the veterinary unit with sanitation audit responsibility.

4. The appropriate public health regulatory authority and purchasing agency will be notified by the unit that selected the destination sample. As applicable, the appropriate food safety office (DSCP consumer safety officer, and so forth) will be notified in the event a recall action is required after the audit.

5. The responsible veterinary unit commander will notify the MACOM veterinarian.

(b) Within 48 hours. Follow the same guidance outlined in paragraph 5–6a(3)(b).

(5) If pathogens or adulterants are discovered in food items from Army food establishments within 24 hours—

(a) The appropriate installation preventive medicine/environmental health (PM/EH) authority will be contacted.

(b) An audit of the producing establishment will be made by the PM/EH unit.

(c) As directed by the director of the MACOM veterinary laboratory, samples of raw ingredients for that particular product will be submitted, as well as end items.

(d) The PM/EH authority will determine the level of medical hold and product/facility suspension needed.

(6) For vendor produced items, if the product fails to obtain three consecutive conforming test results the product, and possibly the entire establishment, remains suspended. A special sanitation audit must be performed to determine sanitation status and continued listing.

b. Samples containing excessive non-pathogenic microbial counts.

(1) If excessive non-pathogenic microbial counts are detected as part of an initial sanitation audit, determination of a food item's approved status will generally be based on the public health risk associated with laboratory results. Final approval authority rests with the MACOM veterinarian.

(2) If excessive non-pathogenic microbial counts are detected as part of the destination monitoring program, a routine sanitation audit may be directed by the MACOM veterinarian. The audit is focused on the particular item and its production method. Veterinary commanders will increase sanitation surveillance as they deem necessary.

(3) If excessive non-pathogenic microbial counts are detected as part of a directed routine or special sanitation audit, determination of a food item's approved status will generally be determined by the public health risk associated with laboratory results. Products that continually show elevated APC/SPC or other non-pathogenic microbial counts may be suspended; the establishment itself may continue to produce under an approved status. No product suspension will be directed by the MACOM under these circumstances without prior conferral with the MACOM laboratory and the procurement agency's food safety/public health authority. Final suspension authority rests with the MACOM veterinarian.

5–7. Suspension of a product or establishment

When a product or establishment is suspended—

a. The MACOM laboratory notifies the—

(1) DVC/Unit commander (origin and destination).

(2) MACOM veterinarian.

(3) Consumer safety officer (ALFOODACTS), HQ DSCP.

b. The DVC/Unit commander responsible for the origin plant notifies the—

(1) Establishment.

(2) Procurement agencies.

(3) MACOM veterinarian (copy of notification letter to establishment).

(4) MACOM laboratory.

(5) Local public health authorities as applicable.

c. The consumer safety officer, DSCP, will issue an ALFOODACT message if necessary.

5–8. Reinstatement procedures for suspended products

a. Reinstatement of an establishments products must be formal and in writing. The contractor must indicate, in writing, to the contracting/purchasing agency, that the cause for suspension has been remedied. This written request is endorsed by the contracting/purchasing agency and forwarded to the DOD Approved Source Division, VETCOM. In addition, documentation of three consecutive conforming laboratory samples must be included in the reinstatement request.

(1) Laboratory samples for reinstatement will be pulled at origin by the establishment, must originate from different production lots than those originally suspended, and must be of the same type/style, flavor, and composition as the suspended products.

(2) Establishments must use an accredited commercial laboratory at their own expense for reinstatement.

b. Once three consecutive conforming test results from an accredited commercial laboratory are verified by the MACOM laboratory, the responsible veterinary command is then notified to perform a directed routine sanitation audit of the establishment and to select laboratory samples from origin to verify absence of pathogens or adulterants.

c. Reinstatement sampling and suspension action will continue until the establishment regains acceptable microbiological/chemical quality. When the MACOM laboratory determines the establishment has regained acceptable quality control, the notification procedures in paragraph 5–6 are again followed.

5–9. Food safety and quality parameters and methods

Laboratory techniques and procedures to determine compliance with this chapter may be found in one or more of the following:

a. Official Methods of Analysis of the Association of Official Analytical Chemists. (http://www.aoac.org/pubs/oma_rev2 htm)

b. FDA's Bacteriological Analytical Manual. (http://vm.cfsan.fda.gov/~ebam/bam-mm html)

c. Compendium of Methods for the Microbiological Examination of Foods, American Public Health Association. (http://www.chipsbooks.com/compend html http://www.scienceb.com/Compendium_of_Methods_for_the_Microbiological_Examination_of_Foods_087553175X html)

d. Standard Methods for the Examination of Dairy Products (http://www.foodsafetysource.com/store/pr detail.cfm?CategoryID=5&ItemID=28&SubCatID=49)

e. Pasteurized Milk Ordinance. (See USPHS Publication No. 229 in Related Publications).

f. USDA Microbiology Laboratory Guide. (http://www.fsis.usda.gov/OPHS/microlab/mlgbook htm)

g. Current methods recognized by applicable Federal regulatory agencies for adulterants and pesticides.

h. ISO/IEC 17025: General Requirements for the Competence of Calibration and Testing Laboratories. (http://www.fasor.com/iso25/)

i. Methods approved by the director, MACOM laboratory.

5–10. Categories of products

Product categories for laboratory analysis are intended to be broad and diverse. Examples are provided regarding type of products found within each category; however, this list of food types is not intended to be all inclusive.

a. Dairy, fresh: Milk and milk products, ice milk mix, dessert mix, soft serve mix.

b. Dairy, frozen: Ice Cream, sherbets, ices, ice milk frozen, novelties, and so forth.

c. Cultured products: Yogurt, sour cream, cottage cheese, buttermilk, acidophilus milk.

d. Prepared salads: Tuna, chicken, turkey, ham, macaroni, potato, cole slaw; spreads, and so forth.

e. Leafy salads/vegetables: Bagged salads, packaged, cut or processed vegetables, and so forth.

f. Sandwiches: Any variety.

g. Ready-to-eat (RTE) meats: Luncheon meat (any variety); pizza toppings; frankfurters (any variety); jerky/meat sticks; sliced meat in jar or bag; and so forth.

h. Ground meat: Coarse or final grind of ground beef, pork, poultry, sausage, and so forth.

i. Cheese: Camembert, feta, cream, ricotta, Brie, Edam, Gouda, Swiss, and so forth.

j. Juice (excluding frozen concentrate): pasteurized or non-pasteurized, any flavor.

k. Fresh seafood: Shrimp, oysters, fresh packaged fish, calamari, modified atmosphere packaged fish, crayfish, scallops, and so forth.

l. Bottled water: In accordance with 21 CFR 165.110 definition.

m. Packaged ice.

n. Other: Kimchee, tofu, dips, and so forth.

Appendix A
References

Section I
Required Publications

AFI 48–116
Food Safety Program. (Cited in the applicability statement and paras 2-1d, 3-3e(2), 3-4e(3), 3-4f, and 3-6.)
http://www.e-publishing.af.mil/pubfiles/af/48/afi48-116/afi48-116.pdf

AR 30–22
The Army Food Program. (Cited in para 3-4e(2) through (3) and 3-4 (3).)

AR 40–656/NAVSUPINST 4355.10/MCO 10110.45
Veterinary Surveillance Inspection of Subsistence. (Cited in paras 3-4 and 3-4(f).)

AR 335–15
Management Information Control System. (Cited in para 2-6e(2).)

Code of Federal Regulations – Title 21, Section 165.110
Bottled Water. (Cited in para 5-10l.)
http://www.access.gpo.gov/nara/cfr/

Code of Federal Regulations – Title 48, Part 246
Quality Assurance. (Cited in para 1-7a.)
http://www.access.gpo.gov/nara/cfr/

Dairy Plants Surveyed and approved for USDA Grading Service
(Cited in para 2-15b(6).) This publication can be obtained from the USDA, Food Safety and Inspection Service,   14th and Independence Avenue, S.W., Washington DC 20250.
http://www.ams.usda.gov/dairy/dypubs.htm

DLAR 4155.26/AR 40–660/NAVSUPINST 10110.8C/AFR 48–116/MCO 10110.38C
DOD Hazardous Food and Nonprescription Drug Recall System. (Cited in para 3-5a.)
http://www.dlaps hq.dla mil

DOD 4160.21–M
Defense Materiel and Disposition Manual. (Cited in para 3-4e(7).)
http://www.dtic mil/whs/directives/corres/pub1 html

DSCPM–4155.6
Nonconformances-Reporting (Subsections 209.1, 218.2, and 218.8). (Cited in para 3-4e(5).) This publication can   be obtained from Defense Supply Center Philadelphia, Directorate of Subsistence, Bldg. 6, ATTN: DSCP-HSL, 700 Robbins Ave., Philadelphia, PA 19111-5092. www.dscp.dla mil/subs

DSCPM –4155.43
Arrival Condition Report Perishable Subsistence. (Cited in para 3-4f.) This publication can be obtained from   Defense Supply Center Philadelphia, Directorate of Subsistence, Bldg. 6, ATTN: DSCP-HSL, 700 Robbins Ave.,   Philadelphia, PA 19111-5092.
www.dscp.dla.mil/subs

FDA Food Code
http://www.cfsan fda.gov/~dms/fc01-toc html

Federal Acquisition Regulation Section 9.106 and its Supplements
(Cited in paras 1-7d and 2-19c.)
http://www.arnet.gov/far/
http://farsite hill.af mil

HACCP Plants Under Federal Inspection
(Cited in paras 2-15a(2)(a).)

http://www.fsis.usda.gov/regulations_&_policies/establishment_specific_information/index.asp

IMS List—Sanitation Compliance and Enforcement Ratings of Interstate Milk Shippers (Published quarterly.)
(Cited in paras 2-6, 2-15a(2)(c), and 4-1c.) This publication can be obtained from the Department of Health and Human Services, Public Health Service, Food and Drug Administration, Milk Safety Branch, HFF-346, 200 C Street, S.W., Washington, DC 20204.
http://www.cfsan.fda.gov

Interstate Certified Shellfish Shippers List
(Cited in table 2-1 and para 2-15a(2)(e).) This publication can be obtained from the Department of Health and Human Services, Shellfish Sanitation, HFF-344, Food and Drug Administration, 200 C St., S.W., Washington, DC 20204.
http://www.cfsan.fda.gov

List of Plants Operating Under USDA Poultry and Egg–Grading and Egg Products Inspection Programs
(Cited in para 2-15a(2)(b).) This publication can be obtained from the USDA, Agricultural Marketing Service, Poultry Division, Grading Branch, 14th and Independence Avenue, S.W., Washington, DC 20250.
http:vets.amedd.army mil.vetcom/index html

MIL–HDBK–3006
Guidelines for Auditing Food Establishments. (Cited in paras 2-2a, 2-4j(1), 2-5e(2), and 2-6e.) This publication can be obtained from Document Automation and Production Service, 700 Robbins Avenue, Bldg. 4, Philadelphia, PA 19111-5094, using DD Form 1435 (Specifications and Standards Requisition).
http://assist1.daps.dla.mil

MIL–STD–904
Detection, Identification, and Prevention of Pest Infestation of Subsistence. (Cited in paras 3-3c, 3-4e(5), and f.) This publication can be obtained from the Document Automation and Production Service, 700 Robbins Avenue, Bldg. 4, Philadelphia, PA 19111-5094, using DD Form 1425 (Specifications and Standards Requisition).

MIL–STD–3006
Sanitation Requirements For Food Establishments. (Cited in paras 2-2a, 2-4b, and 3-7c.) This publication can be obtained from the Document Automation and Production Service, 700 Robbins Avenue, Bldg. 4, Philadelphia, PA 19111-5094, using DD Form 1435 (Specifications and Standards Requisition).

NAVMED P–5010
Manual of Naval Preventive Medicine. (Cited in para 3-3e(1)(a).)
http://www-nehc.med.navy mil

NAVSUP P–486
Food Service Management of General Messes. (Cited in para 3-3e(1)(a), 3-4d(3)(a)4, and 3-4e(2).)
http://www.cpp.usmc.mil/tenant/wcfmt/publications/p486ch1%20TO%204.pdf

TB MED 263
Medical Service, Identification of Inspected Foods. (Cited in paras 2-4i, 3-3f(2), and 3-6.)

USDC Approved List of Fish Establishments and Products
(Cited in para 2-15a(2)(d).) This publication can be obtained from USDC, P.O. Drawer 1207, Pascagoula, MS 39567-0112.
http://seafood nmfs noaa.gov/publications.htm,
http://vets.amedd.army.mil/vetcom/index html

Veterinary Command Food Analysis and Diagnostic Laboratory Submission Guide
(Cited in para 4-4.)
http://vets.amedd.army.mil/vetlab/GUIDE.pdf

Worldwide Directory

A Directory of Sanitarily Approved Food Establishments for Armed Forces Procurement (Cited in paras 1-4a(5); 1-4a(11); 1-4b(1)(c); 1-4b(1)(d); 1-4b(2)(b); 2-1; 2-4a; 2-4c; 2-4j; 2-4j(2); 2-6a; 2-6c(2); 2-6c(3); 2-6d; 2-12a; 2-12b; 2-12c(2); 2-12c(4); 2-13a; 2-14a; 2-14b; 2-14e; 2-15; 2-15a(2); 2-15a(2)(g); 2-15a(2)(i); 2-15b; 2-16; 5-1; 5-3a; and 5-6a(3)(b)1.) This publication can be obtained from Commander, U.S. Army Veterinary Command, ATTN: MCVS-FA, Fort Sam Houston, TX 78234-6000. Overseas MACOMs will provide their own Directory annex for OCONUS establishments outside the jurisdiction of VETCOM.
http://vets.amedd.army.mil/vetcom/index.html

Section II
Related Publications

A related publication is merely a source of additional information. The user does not have to read it to understand this regulation.

AR 11–2
Management Control

AR 25–50
Preparing and Managing Correspondence

AR 40–1
Composition, Mission, and Functions of the Army Medical Department

AR 40–3
Medical, Dental, and Veterinary Care

AR 40–4
Army Medical Department Facilities/Activities

AR 40–5
Preventive Medicine

AR 40–905/SECNAVINST 6401.1 A/AFI 48–135
Veterinary Health Services

AR 702–18/DLAR 4155.37/NAVSUPINST4410.56A; AFMAN 23–110; MCO 4450.13
Material Quality Storage Standards Policy for Shelf-Life Materiel: Appendix S--Subsistence

DODI 4000.19
Inter-Service and Intra-Governmental Support. This publication and all standards and the handbook listed below may be obtained from the Document Automation and Production Service, 700 Robbins Avenue, Bldg. 4, Philadelphia, PA 19111-5094
www.dtic.mil/whs/directives

DSCPH 4155.2
Inspection of Composite Operational Rations. This publication can be obtained from Defense Supply Center Philadelphia, Directorate of Subsistence, Bldg. 6, ATTN: DSCP-HSL, 700 Robbins Ave., Philadelphia, PA 19111-5092.
http://www.dscp.dla mil/subs/subsbo/qapubs/HBK41552.pdf

DSCPM 4155.7
Perishable Subsistence-In-Storage Quality Control and Inspection. This publication can be obtained from Defense Supply Center Philadelphia, Directorate of Subsistence, Bldg. 6, ATTN: DSCP-HSL, 700 Robbins Ave., Philadelphia, PA 19111-5092.
http://www.dscp.dla mil/subs/subsbo/qapubs/4155-7.pdf

ESR 1–2
Veterinary and Preventive Medicine Services. This publication can be obtained from Headquarters, Army and Air Force Exchange Service, ATTN: Staff Veterinarian, Dallas, TX 75266-0202.

FDA Investigations Operations Manual

http://www.ntis.gov/products/pages/fda-iom.asp

Humane Methods of Slaughter Act, Public Law 95–445

http://www.gpoaccess.gov/plaws/index html

Journal of Food Protection

Publications 3A (Sanitary Standards and Accepted Practices) and E-3-A (Sanitary Standards (Eggs)) These publications can be obtained from the Journal of Food Protection, P.O. Box 701, Ames IA 50010 or   http://www.techstreet.com/3Agate html

MEDCOM Regulation 40–28

Veterinary Standardization Policies and Procedures. www.dscp.dla mil

MIL–HDBK 154

Inspection of Fruit and Vegetable Farms and Packing Sheds in Overseas Areas http://assist1.daps.dla mil

TM 38–400/NAVSUP PUB 572/AFMAN 23–210/MCO 4450–14/DLAM 4145.12

Joint Service Manual (JSM) for Storage and Materials Handling

TB MED 530

Occupational and Environmental Health: Food Sanitation.

USDA Meat Inspection Regulation (Part 327)—Imported Products

This publication can be obtained from USDA, Meat and Poultry Inspection, 0157 South Building, 14th and Independence Avenue, S.W., Washington, DC 20250. http://www.access.gpo.gov/nara/cfr/waisidx_04/9cfr327_04 html

USPHS Publication No. 33

National Shellfish Sanitation Service Publication Program Manual of Operations
Part I: Control of Shellfish Growing Areas
Part II: Sanitation of the Harvesting and Processing of Shellfish, US Department of Health and Human   Services. These can be obtained from Department of Health and Human Services, Public Health Service, Food and Drug Administration, Shellfish Sanitation Branch, HFF-344, 200 C Street, S.W., Washington, DC 20204. http://vm.cfsan fda.gov/~ear/nsspman html

USPHS Publication No. 229

Grade "A" Pasteurized Milk Ordinance, US Department of Health and Human Services. This publication can be obtained from HQDA (DASG-VCP), 5109 Leesburg Pike, Falls Church, VA 22041-3258. http://www.cfsan.fda.gov/~acrobat/pmo01.pdf

U.S. Post Office Publication No. 65

National Five-digit ZIP Code and Post Office Directory. This publication can be obtained at local post offices.

Section III

Unless otherwise stated, DA forms are available on the Army Publishing Directorate web site (www.apd.army.mil), and DD forms are available from the OSD Web site (http://www.dtic.mil/whs/directives/informgt/forms/fromsprogram htm).

DA Form 7538

Subsistence Serviceability Certificate. (Prescribed in paragraph 3–4e(3).)

DA Form 7539

Request for Veterinary Laboratory Testing and Food Sample Record. (Prescribed in paragraph 4–4b.)

DD Form 2385

Microbial Quality History Record. (Prescribed in paragraph 5-5b(4).)

Section IV
Referenced Forms

DA Form 11–2–R
Management Control Evaluation Certification Statement

DA Form 2028
Recommended Changes to Publications and Blank Forms

DD Form 1222
Request for and Results of Tests

DD Form 1232
Quality Assurance Representative's Correspondence

DD Form 1425
Specifications and Standards Requisition

Appendix B
Army Veterinary Service Geographic Areas of Responsibility

B–1. Overview
Personnel of the Army available for inspections may be obtained from the addressees listed by area in table B–1.

B–2. Requests
The requests for these services should contain all contractual or other pertinent information necessary for conducting them. Sanitation audit requests for CONUS establishments must be signed by the plant owner or authorized representative and sent to the military purchasing activity for evaluation and forwarding to the Commander, U.S. Army Veterinary Command, ATTN: MCVS–FA, Fort Sam Houston, TX 78234–6005.

B–3. Central procurement food inspections
When inspection of foods incident to the central procurement is desired, the request should be submitted in duplicate, through command channels to the appropriate Service, directly to the appropriate addressee. Each request for food inspection should state the class or classes of inspection desired, as defined in table 2–1. If inspections are desired before printed copies of the purchase instrument are available for distribution, the written inspection request should incorporate all contractual information necessary to accomplish the requested inspections.

Table B–1
U.S. Army Veterinary Service Geographic Areas of Responsibility

Addressee	Area Commander
U.S. Army Veterinary Command ATTN: MCVS-FA Fort Sam Houston, TX 78234-6005 AUTOVON: 471-6547/6524 Commercial: (210) 221-6547/6524	Continental U.S. plus North Atlantic and Car bbean areas as designated by VETCOM Commander. All points in Alaska, and points in the Pacific Theater and Southeast Asia, except South Korea. All points in Central and South America.
Commander U.S. Forces Korea ATTN: EAMC-Vet, Unit 15252 APO AP 96205-0025	All points in South Korea.
Commander USAREUR & 7th Army Unit #29351 ATTN: AEAMD-VS APO AE 09014	All points in USEUCOM's area of responsibility including Greenland and Iceland.
Veterinary Services PSC 451, Box VET FPO AE 09834-2800	All points in USCENTCOM's area of responsibility.

Appendix C
Management Control Evaluation

C–1. Function
The function covered by this evaluation is the Inspection of Food Establishments and the Laboratory Sampling Program process. The checklist includes key controls for the sanitation audit program, receipt inspections, surveillance inspections, and the laboratory monitoring programs.

C–2. Purpose
The purpose of this evaluation is to assist in evaluating the key management controls listed below. This evaluation should be used at the following level: INSTL. It is not intended to cover all controls, but you must evaluate all of the controls applicable to your activity

C–3. Instructions
Answers must be based on the actual testing of key management controls (that is, document analysis, direct observation, sampling, simulation, other). Answers that indicate deficiencies must be explained and corrective action indicated in supporting documentation. These key management controls must be formally evaluated at least once every five years. Document certification on DA Form 11–2–R (Management Control Evaluation Certification Statement). This form is available on the APD Web site.

C–4. Test Questions
    a. Are the military and commercial sanitation audit programs operating correctly, utilizing proper personnel (para 2–1), frequencies (para 2–6), and correct documents and procedures (para 2–2)?

    b. Are origin acceptance, ante-mortem and post-mortem inspection programs operating correctly (para 3–2)?

    c. Is a documented support plan developed and maintained properly (para 3–3)?

    d. Are receipt inspections being performed properly, to include documentation and reporting (para 3–3)?

    e. Are surveillance inspections being performed properly, to include documentation and reporting (para 3–4)?

    f. Are approved source requirements being checked properly (para 3–3)?

    g. Are Prime Vendor Product Compliance Evaluations conducted correctly (para 3–4d(4))?

    h. Are ALFOODACT inspections made in accordance with DLAR 4155.6/AR 40–660/NAVSUPINST 10110.8/AFR 48–116/MCO 10110.38 (para 3–5)?

    i. Are the appropriate military laboratories being utilized properly (para 4–1)?

    j. Are procedures for product sampling during sanitation audits being followed correctly (para 5–5a)?

    k. Are procedures for product sampling during destination monitoring being followed correctly (para 5–5b)?

C–4. Supersession
There were no previous evaluations.

C–5. Comments
Help to make this a better tool for evaluation management controls. Submit comments to: DODVSA/OTSG, 5109 Leesburg Pike, Falls Church, VA 22041–3258.

Glossary

Section I
Abbreviations

AAFES
Army and Air Force Exchange Service

ACES
Army Center of Excellence Subsistence

AOR
area of responsibility

ALFOODACT
All Food/Drug Activities

AMEDDC&S
United States Army Medical Department Center and School

AMS
Agricultural Marketing Service

APC
aerobic plate counts

APF
appropriated funds

ARNG
Army National Guard

CAR
Corrective Action Request

CDR
commander

CFR
Code of Federal Regulations

CONUS
continental United States

DAF
Department of the Air Force

DECA
Defense Commissary Agency

DLA
Defense Logistics Agency

DODVSA
Department of Defense Veterinary Service Activity

DRMO
Defense Reutilization and Marketing Office

DSCP
Defense Supply Center Philadelphia

DVC
District Veterinary Command

DVM
Doctor of Veterinary Medicine

EH
environmental health

FAR
Federal Acquisition Regulation

FDA
Food and Drug Administration

FOB
free on board

FREC
Food Risk Evaluation Committee

FSC
Federal supply classification

FSIS
Food Safety Inspection Service

FSSV
food safety surveillance visits

FWSC
Food and Water Safety Committee

HACCP
hazard analysis and critical control points

HQDA
Headquarters, Department of Army

ICSSL
Interstate Certified Shellfish Shippers List

IMS
Interstate Milk Shippers

IMSL
Interstate Milk Shippers List

IRC
inspection responsibility code

MACOM
major Army command

MOS
military occupational specialty

MWR
morale, welfare, and recreation

MRE
meal, ready-to-eat

NAF
nonappropriated funds

NCO
noncommissioned officer

NEX
Navy exchange

OCONUS
outside continental United States

OTSG
Office of The Surgeon General

PCE
product compliance evaluation

PHF
potentially hazardous food

PM
preventive medicine

PV
prime vendor

QA
quality assurance

RTE
ready-to-eat

RVC
Regional Veterinary Command

SGM
sergeant major

SPC
standard plate counts

SSG
staff sergeant

TSG
The Surgeon General

UBL
unit basic loads

UGR
unitized group ration

UGR–A
unitized group ration - A

USA
United States Army

USAF
United States Air Force

USAR
United States Army Reserves

USDA
United States Department of Agriculture

USDC
United States Department of Commerce

USMC
United States Marine Corps

USN
United States Navy

USPHS
United States Public Health Service

WO
warrant officer

VCO
Veterinary Corps officer

VMD
Veterinary Medicine Doctor

VETCOM
United States Army Veterinary Command

Section II
Terms

Depot
An activity for the receipt, issue, storage, or supply of semiperishable food for more than one military installation.

Food establishments and facilities
Premises, buildings, equipment, and vehicles used by civilian suppliers (wholesale) to handle, process, manufacture, assemble, store, freeze, or transport foods. Normally, this term does not include food service establishments such as restaurants, snack bars and dining facilities, or facilities engaged in retail marketing (such as meat markets or civilian grocery stores) except when the retail marketing facilities are operating on a military installation.

Grand lotting
Collecting or grouping two or more lots of like quality in order to decrease the cost of surveillance inspections by reducing the number of samples.

Inactive establishments
Establishments that no longer actively supply the Armed Forces or NAF activities.

Imminent health hazard
A product or practice that creates or appears to create a significant threat or danger to health that must be corrected immediately.

Perishable

A subsistence item that normally requires refrigeration for storage.

Port

Places and activities normally associated with sea or aerial transportation services.

Procurement agency

The requiring activity.

Sanitation audit

An inspection to determine the sanitary conditions of food establishments and facilities.

Semiperishable

A subsistence item that normally does not require refrigeration for storage.

Serviceability

The fitness of a subsistence item for its intended purpose.

Section III
Special Abbreviations and Terms

This section contains no entries.